SUSTAINABLE Living & MINDFUL Eating

Lisa Schmidt
Arizona State University

Kendall Hunt
publishing company

4 Step MAC logo art by Heather Crank. Copyright © 2015 by Maria Napoli.

Mindful Eating: Practicing the 4 Step MAC Guide CD is copyright © 2015 by Maria Napoli and Susan Busatti Giangano. It is reprinted with this book by permission.

Cover image courtesy of Maria Napoli.

Kendall Hunt
publishing company

www.kendallhunt.com
Send all inquiries to:
4050 Westmark Drive
Dubuque, IA 52004-1840

Contents

About the Author

Lisa Schmidt, MS, CN, CEBS, CYT, is a Faculty Associate at the Arizona State University Integrative Health Initiatives Program where she teaches courses on mindfulness skills for stress management. As a Certified Nutritionist, mindfulness consultant, mental health counselor, and Certified Yoga Teacher (CYT) in private practice, she supports whole person health throughout the lifespan teaching healthful eating and stress management using science-based mind–body interventions. Ms. Schmidt has incorporated the practice of mindfulness in corporate employee benefits design, and consults and speaks internationally with companies and as a conference presenter. Ms. Schmidt is the owner of Mindful Benefits, which provides tools and practices that enhance the way we live and encourages non-judgment, kindness, curiosity, and compassion leading to changing longstanding habits that impact our health. She is a graduate of Bastyr University, with dual MS degrees in Nutrition and Clinical Health Psychology, and a Certified Employee Benefits Professional (CEBS).

Introduction

> "We've been so disconnected agriculturally and culturally from food.
> We spend more time on dieting than on cooking."
> —*Alice Waters*

Mindfulness means paying attention to the present moment with non-judgment, curiosity, and kindness. Mindfulness as a practice offers the possibility of becoming aware of the interconnection of the Earth, living beings, cultural practices and the impact of our food choices on those systems. Sustainable Living & Mindful Eating is a book designed to move you toward connection. Connection to others and the world around us requires responsibility and presence. As we imagine our interrelationship with all living beings and the world, we may develop perspectives supporting a new and different relationship with the environment. Food becomes more than a recreational activity, and eating is elevated beyond something to "do" when bored, lonely, tired, anxious, worried, or depressed. Our connection or lack of connection to food and its energetic properties defines us, aligns our relationship with the world and its inhabitants and offers us the possibility of freedom, guided by the practice of Mindfulness.

Mindfulness has been compared to concepts related to flow, being in the moment, or even living in the now. There is an important differentiation when we think about the ancient practice of mindfulness that for thousands of years has been as a form of spiritual connection and mental training. Mindfulness requires a certain type of awareness. It is not simply enough to just decide to pay attention. Rather, with our minds and lives distracted by the nature of modern living, we decide <u>with intention</u> to practice paying attention to the present moment. Mindfulness practice helps us connect to what is right in front of us, which many find an impossible task. Constantly distracted by technology, we rush around from activity to activity disconnected from our bodies, our surroundings, our nourishment, and our lives. Acting as if on automatic pilot, our stressed out lives encourage mindless eating, munching away by habit on highly palatable, high calorie, nutritionally poor foods. As a result, stress- related disorders (including obesity from "over nutrition") now account for 60 to 90 percent of all doctors' visits, as estimated by the Benson-Henry institute.

Our distraction leads to modern diseases of excess; in particular, our disconnection to food and eating has led to an obesity epidemic. In our humanness, we search externally for things to blame. We blame the food companies, who make the calorie dense, nutritionally poor processed food; fast food outlets, who serve huge portions of poor quality food at minimal prices; even advertising, which cultivates taste and desire preferences even from an early age (you'll read how this is intentionally done to influence children as consumers for life in Chapter 6). Modern conveniences might be to blame, since they limit movement and suppress our daily calorie burn. Some even blame things like gluten and carbohydrates, advocating a return to our primitive, caveman roots with a prehistoric dietary approach.

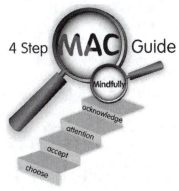

It is almost a radical act to look inward for explanations of our distress towards food and nourishment. Sustainable Living & Mindful Eating is my invitation to you to look inward. It is my response to those who claim that eating well is simply too confusing, too difficult, and not that important.

I will show you how we can repair our difficulties with food and eating by connecting through mindfulness practice. We can by paying attention and noticing what is right in front of us, start to notice the effects of different food. We can learn satisfaction from the actual energy provided by food by reconnecting with how we feel when we eat different things. Through knowledge of the manufacturing of processed and fast food, we can begin to question our assumptions and elevate the importance of food in our lives.

As we connect with our mindfulness practice to all living beings, I'll suggest that you give your food a face. In other words, instead of thinking about food as shrink wrapped, purified, sanitized packages of animal protein, I'll encourage you to consider the sentient being that you're about to eat. I'll invite you to consider how that animal was treated as it was raised for your consumption, and if it was permitted a noble passing. You'll learn the real price of a cheap hamburger in our country where mass produced meat, chicken and pork is BIG business. Don't worry, I won't define what to eat and what to avoid – this is not a diet book or a judgment about you or your eating habits. Rather, through connection, information and facts I'd like you to consider for perhaps the first time in your life if WHAT you eat aligns with who you are and who you hope to be. Through our conversation about food, nourishment, and vitality, you'll find for yourself a recipe for lifetime satisfaction!

We live during a time when modern medicine declares that there is no such prescription as "one size fits all." Our culture is one of scientific reductionism where scientists spend their careers closely examining very small areas of knowledge. Our disease system views humans as "parts" and each disease is considered separate from the "whole person". Instead of health care, we have a system of disease management. We are removed from knowing the body as an integrated system where all elements interact with, and influence, each other. You'll learn how to view the body differently, as an integrated whole organism, with its innate ability to self-regulate and move to balance. This ancient wisdom conflicts with our modern approach to medicine that treats each disease separately, and we respond with prescriptions for each ailment. We have forgotten the one solution which for thousands of years has proven effective to treat multiple ailments – what we eat, and how we eat, since both matter. Treating diseases individually through the idea that each has its own specific cause, its own unique pathway, and its own-targeted cure (usually a prescription medication) encourages a narrow focus. What if instead we paid attention to the overlapping relationship between causes, mechanisms and outcomes? What if we considered that nutrition had a major role in what ails us? How might things change?

It is clear that poor nutrition causes more diseases than the disease-care system currently acknowledges, and good nutrition is a cure for many diseases, maybe all. Poor nutrition is now implicated in many, if not all, medical conditions, especially those like cardiovascular disease, diabetes, hypertension, and digestive problems that are considered "lifestyle related" diseases.

The solution to what ails us is the ancient practice of mindfulness, with its focus on embracing each moment of our lives and learning how to simply notice. Thousands of clinical studies done in health care settings suggest the tremendous power of mindfulness practice to heal a myriad of health conditions. Isn't it remarkable that the practice of noticing, first using the breath, body sensations, and moving into thoughts and feelings without judgment can produce such amazing health benefits?

Sustainable Living & Mindful Eating will offer you an opportunity to reflect on the food you eat, where it comes from, how you eat and what happens in your body the moment you take a mouthful. Your eating experience will most likely change for life as you mindfully acknowledge your current patterns of nutrition. You'll pay attention how you choose the food you eat and when you eat. You'll be encouraged to accept your experiences and decisions without judgment and, if appropriate for you, take action to make a choice for change. Be gentle with yourself and take time to absorb the information shared with you in this book, as you will most likely find that change needs to take place in your life. Mindfulness asks that we take small steps as we become aware of the changes we need to make, take time to practice and develop new behaviors and attitudes toward our nutrition and finally, begin to integrate healthy and nutritious behaviors that will improve the quality of our lives and the world around us.

Once we notice we have a choice to change. The opportunity to live more fully in tune with the environment, eating mindfully with awareness, and in harmony with our body rhythms gives us a sustainable approach to nourishment and life. Sustainable Living & Mindful Eating brings these practices to us with the possibility of fully embracing the life we are meant to live. Enjoy this book bite by bite, and breathe in the awareness that mindfulness and ease is your birthright.

Sustainable Living, Mindful Eating

Courtesy of Maria Napoli

Simple beauty
The silence of gazing
Slowing chewing my food
No rush
My body feels gratitude
Savoring each and every bite
On this mindful eating journey

(Napoli)

> "Let food be your medicine and medicine be your food."
> —Hippocrates (460–530 B.C.)

The father of modern medicine scribed these words nearly 2,500 years ago. The words of Hippocrates have been used to communicate how a connection with nature through a relationship with food can provide health benefits far beyond any other type of "prescription". Seen through this lens, eating is an intimate way to extract life-sustaining energy from Mother Nature. The primary, ongoing way that we consciously or unconsciously relate to nature is through our food. Through the act of food consumption (eating), we assimilate the forces of nature, stored in our food (1). This transformation of stored energy into released energy providing fuel for our bodies is magical, amazing, and powerful!

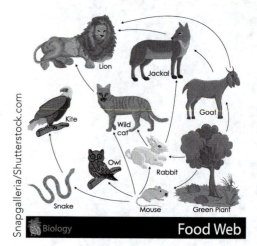

Food Web

Snapgalleria/Shutterstock.com

Energy passes from one animal to another as they eat plants or one another. This flow of energy from one living thing to another is called a food chain or a food web (2). When we think of energy exchanges in this way, we can see the interconnections we have to plants and animals, and to the energy of nature itself. When we allow ourselves to see all living beings as part of an interconnected web, we can enhance and move toward a changed view of food and the act of eating. Nourishment becomes much more than just about what you and your family eats for dinner; it is also about the ripples that result from the need to eat, our connections to the entire world, and all inhabitants. We connect as links in the enormous food chain, and our lives depend upon our love and gratitude for all other links (3). What we eat is linked to our awareness, and our food choices show our harmony (or disharmony) with our communities, the world, and ourselves.

DISCONNECTION AND DISHARMONY: MODERN AILMENTS?

All humans have an intrinsic, organic relationship with these fundamental elements, and disease is an outgrowth of a deficiency of one or more of them. Obesity, diabetes, and other conditions caused by poor diet and sedentary lifestyle is one consequence of disconnection to nature and food energetics.

TAGSTOCK1/Shutterstock.com

There is a crisis of health underway which affects the health, happiness, and vitality of millions of men, women, and, sadly, children in the United States. Instead of national action to face these threats, there has been thunderous inaction, and even surrender to a powerful food industry (4). The obesity problem has been labeled by national agencies as "epidemic" (5). Within the United States, the current percentage of Americans considered overweight or obese is more than 68% (6). The good news is the numbers have plateaued—the bad news is the bigger the number, the harder it becomes mathematically to continue to climb. If things continue as they are, we face a staggering financial burden due to obesity-related illnesses.

In the United States, obesity now contributes more to chronic illness and health care costs than does smoking (7,8).

National Problem Becomes Personal Frustration

Although we have wide awareness of the national problem of obesity, we can forget the personal frustration and suffering caused from being overweight in the United States. It seems impossible to lose weight with dismal statistics showing that 95% of all dieting attempts result in abandonment with dieters regaining lost weight plus more from the starting point of the diet (9). Everywhere we turn there is evidence of both the conditions and the consequences of a weight-focused culture. Experts call the toxicity of our modern culture "obesogenic" (10). Societal forces that drive us to eat more and move less surround us. Biologically, this results in weight gain, obesity, and the many health problems and consequences of an unhealthy lifestyle. Conflicting information directs us to solve the problem in many ways; blame ourselves/personal responsibility (just eat less and move more); blame the food companies (regulate and tax junk food; restrict food advertising to kids); blame the environment (the Internet, our work life, television all cause us to sit more and move less); blame food science (high-salt, high-sugar, high-fat processed foods make us eat more and gain weight); or blame the diet business (dieting leads to weight gain 95% of the time; scientific evidence fails to support any rigid diet plans work).

Disordered Eating in the Land of Plenty

The obesity problem is one consequence of living in the land of plenty. Disordered eating in our culture can be overconsumption of calories, under consumption, or even a zealous fixation on eating "clean". Some react to abundance by learning about food, and falling to the other extreme in ways that are equally disordered. Experts call this unhealthy way of eating healthy orthorexia (11).

Orthorexic eating can become almost like a religion, with a position instead of a preference. People might refuse to eat "gluten", may be over focused on eating "clean" ingredients, even refusing social commitments if the "right" kind of food is not available. At the extreme, an orthorexic person might skip a cruise vacation if they don't think they'll like the food on the ship.

The Modern Food System and Reductionism

Modern changes such as the development of the industrialized food system have changed the role of food in our lives. It has also led to changes in how we think and feel about food. Instead of contemplating the healing and nourishing properties of food and eating, the industrialized process of food production disconnects us from plants and animals. Today we consider health as just getting through

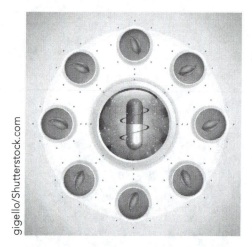

gigello/Shutterstock.com

the day, making a living, or not dropping dead. We believe that good health is the absence of disease. We look at the body as disconnected parts and pieces, we see many different doctors, one for each body part (the ear doctor, the heart doctor, the orthopedic doctor, the skin doctor). When something goes wrong in the body, instead of seeing our bodies as an integrated system, we view the disease in isolation and disconnect from our whole selves. Our model of disease and health as influenced by Modern science sees smaller and smaller parts of ourselves, bits and pieces, in order to solve the puzzle of disease. Not health . . . the disease.

We have convinced ourselves that our health has nothing to do with what we eat. We spend lots of money and time buying the best toys and gadgets of top quality, and when it comes to what we eat or put in our bodies we run to the nearest fast food restaurant because it is easy. It's convenient. We think cooking and preparing food is just too complicated and time consuming! As a consequence, we have created a separation between food and illness in our culture.

Food Energetics: Why It Matters

The process of thinking about a disease system disconnects us from the energetics and function of food. In a process known as "reductionism" we think of food as "nutrients"—this much protein, this much iron, and this much fiber—small units of food that come from science, and the laboratory (12). For thousands of years, Ancient Wisdom viewed food differently, and studied its energetic properties. Each person was seen as an individual, and with individual constitutions, each person has their own needs for certain foods. Remedies for ailments used herbs in their whole form, often steeped in water and often as one of several ingredients (13).

Food then becomes much more than fuel, it moves beyond the science and mechanics of calories, grams, and nutrients. Food energetics matches the properties and qualities of the plant or animal—the grounded nature of root vegetables, the warming or cooling qualities of different foods—as nutritional prescriptions to help balance the body.

Hein Nouwens/Shutterstock.com

Vareennik/Shutterstock.com

MINDFULNESS AND SUSTAINABILITY

As humans, we have the innate ability to seek out and enjoy foods that promote our health. Consuming mostly plant-based foods in their "whole" form (close to their natural state) provides the ideal human diet (14). Eating a variety of vegetables, fruits, raw nuts and seeds, beans and legumes, and whole grains provides all of the nutritional needs that humans have. These whole foods, mostly plant-based prescription, are likely close to the medicine that Hippocrates pondered nearly 3,000 years ago.

> "Eat food. Not too much. Mostly plants."
> —*Michael Pollan*

Michael Pollan, the food philosopher of our time, brings us closer to Hippocrates with his modern description of what is the optimal diet (15). He suggests that we don't eat anything that our great grandmother wouldn't recognize; don't eat anything incapable of rotting; avoid food that has ingredients that cannot be understood or pronounced, or has more than five ingredients; don't eat high fructose corn syrup; avoid food products that make health claims; that we shop the peripheries of supermarkets, and avoid them as much as possible; that we eat mostly plants, especially leaves; and that we remember that we are what we eat, and that we eat eats too. Which means it is not just what we eat, but the quality of the food we eat that matters. Energetically, it also means *how we eat* matters as

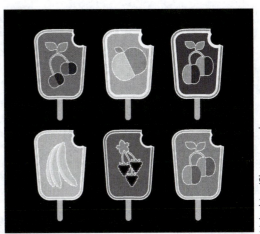

Voloshina/Shutterstock.com

well—mindfully, in harmony with nature, aware, awake, and alive, honoring where our food came from. In short, a balanced approach that considers energetics, tastes, quality, variety, mindfulness and balance.

It is difficult for us to understand that food itself is good for us. We live in a world where science attempts to dissect, and then explain the "active ingredients" of food, rather than simply accept it is the whole food that has medicinal benefits. This approach, called reductionism (16), asks for the impossible, since it is simply not possible to identify all the parts, what they do, and how they work together or individually. We can, however, know that food is healing, and it is magical. Thousands of years of using food medicinally combined with current scientific research demonstrate over and over that it is a whole food, mostly plant-based diet that heals, not the dissected parts.

> "Nature does a far better job of arranging for proper biological functioning than we like to admit, and once we accept the ability of the body's infinitely complex system to attain and maintain health, then the one-size fits all philosophy begins to make sense (17)."

We can imagine "one size" being whole, plant-based foods, with an almost infinite number and variety of parts acting synergistically as one, with "fits all" meaning food has the ability to act to promote and preserve health, and help heal multiple illnesses. This is a useful and powerful way to view food and its energetics, which aligns Ancient Wisdom and what we know about plants with the benefits of a whole foods mostly plant-based diet. Assimilation takes the energy that is locked up in food and releases it. This transformed energetics from plants and animals becomes the fuel that sustains our own lives and we become nourished through this natural and magical process. Each bite, if we choose to consciously acknowledge the transformation, can bring us closer to our loving connection with Mother Nature.

Sustainable Living, Mindful Eating: The Cure for What Ails Us?

The practice of mindfulness is paying attention to the present moment, without judgment. Mindfulness offers the cultivated ability to notice thoughts, habits of mind, and habits of body in ways that allow us to see what is happening right in front of us. Stopping allows us to rest the body and the mind. Looking deeply inside provides insight into our current situation. Once we notice, we can attempt the process of change in ways that are aligned with our values, circumstances, and connections to all living beings. Rather than blaming external forces and conditions for our inability to change our weight, we begin to cultivate positive habits of mind leading to sustainable eating and life patterns providing true nourishment (18).

> "The federal committee responsible for nutrition guidelines is calling for the adoption of 'plant-based' diets, taxes on dessert, trained obesity 'interventionists' at worksites, and electronic monitoring of how long Americans sit in front of the television (19)."

Sustainable Living, Mindful Eating: A Journey Back Home

We're about to embark on a journey together that may challenge your assumptions about food, the act of eating, and its importance. Be curious, gentle, and kind with yourself as you travel. It can be difficult to examine our assumptions and givens about the personal act of food and eating. We can carry with us on our journey the practice of mindfulness and its tremendous benefits. You'll be invited to pause and breathe as you read this book, noticing your body, thoughts, and qualities of breath. You'll be introduced to mindful nutrition tips in the form of recipes, mindful eating activities, and other simple practices designed to help you reflect and pause. You'll learn about different aspects of our food system that many consider broken and unsustainable (20). Some of this information will be new and may be troubling; it is powerful stuff. Remember to be kind, curious, and gentle with your journey. Feel your body and your breath as you embark on your travels, always remembering that knowing is part of mindfulness: once we notice, we have the opportunity to change.

MINDFUL EATING: THE MODERN PRESCRIPTION

High-speed living moves much of our eating to autopilot. We do not pay attention to how much food is served or how much we've eaten, what our food tastes like, what it's made from, or even if we like it! This means we've lost touch with cues reflecting hunger or fullness. Mindlessly eating meal after meal, snack after snack, we fall victim to portion distortion, poor food quality, and mindless munching. We think little about the quality or quantity of our food. We pop processed "food like substances" into our microwaves, dashing from one activity to another.

Cues for mindless eating reach beyond super-sized containers and the sizes of our plates. Our food environment through advertising and endless exposure encourages fast food consumption of poor quality food, purchasing highly processed "dead" food from the supermarkets and 24-hour snacking. All of these cues combined with our hectic lifestyles encourage mindless eating without regard for what our bodies truly need.

Practicing mindfulness can help us notice the external cues that keep us trapped in patterns of unsustainable mindless eating. Instead, through paying attention and noticing with curiosity, we can find new ways of nourishment though healthful foods that are sustainable, delicious, and truly satisfying. The practice of eating mindfully provides endless opportunities for self-exploration, discovery, and ultimately joy as we reconnect to the nourishing powers and energetics of plants and their special healing energetics.

Let's Reflect on the Mindful MAC FOUR STEP Guide

BEGIN YOUR MINDFUL EATING AND DRINKING EXPERIENCE USING THE MAC GUIDE SAVORING AND NOTICING EACH STEP FROM BEGINNING TO END

Maglara/Shutterstock.com

Mindful Eating Practice

The next time you sit down for a meal, use your utensil with your nondominant hand. Notice the weight of your silverware as you pay attention to what it feels like to use your other hand for eating. Does it allow you to pay more attention to your food? Slow down your pace of eating? Breathe—notice—be curious and gentle as this simple practice reconnects you with your food.

Journal your reflections here:

_____

_____

_____

_____

_____

References

1. Cousins, G. 2000. *Conscious Eating.* Berkeley, CA: North Atlantic Books.
2. Idaho Public Television. 2015. "Food Web Facts." Available from: http://idahoptv.org/sciencetrek/topics/food_chain/facts.cfm.
3. Schmidt, L. 2014. "Sustainable Living and Conscious Eating." In *Beyond Stress: Strategies for Blissful Living,* ed. Napoli, M., p. 55. Dubuque, IA: Kendall Hunt.
4. Brownell, K. D. and Horgen, K. B. 2004. *Food Fight: The Inside Story of the Food Industry, America's Obesity Crisis, and What We Can Do About It.* Chicago: Contemporary Books.
5. Centers for Disease Control and Prevention. 2011. "Obesity and Overweight: A Public Health Epidemic." CDC website. [February 22, 2015]. Available from: http://www.cdc.gov/cdctv/diseaseandconditions/lifestyle/obesity-epidemic.html.
6. Food Research and Action Center. 2010. "Overweight and Obesity in the U.S." Available from: http://frac.org/initiatives/hunger-and-obesity/obesity-in-the-us/.
7. O'Grady, M. J. and Capretta, J. C. (2012). "Assessing the Economics of Obesity and Obesity Interventions." Campaign to End Obesity. Available from: http://www.rwjf.org/en/about-rwjf/newsroom/newsroom-content/2012/03/new-report-shows-importance-of-calculating-full-cost-savings-of-.html.
8. Robert Wood Johnson Foundation. 2014. "Cost Containment and Obesity Prevention." Available from: http://stateofobesity.org/cost-containment/.
9. UCLA Newsroom. 2007. "Dieting Does Not Work, UCLA Researchers Report." Available from: http://newsroom.ucla.edu/releases/Dieting-Does-Not-Work-UCLA-Researchers-7832.
10. Hyman, M. 2010. "The Toxic Triad: How Big Food, Big Farming, and Big Pharma Spread Obesity, Diabetes, and Chronic Disease Across the Globe." Available from: http://drhyman.com/blog/2010/10/22/the-toxic-triad-how-big-food-big-farming-and-big-pharma-spread-obesity-diabetes-and-chronic-disease-across-the-globe/.
11. Kratina, K. 2014. "Orthorexia Nervosa." *NEDA.* Available from: https://www.nationaleatingdisorders.org/orthorexia-nervosa.
12. Campbell, T. C. (2013). *Whole. Rethinking the Science of Nutrition.* Dallas, TX: Benbella Books.
13. Sekhar, M., Aneesh, T., Varghese, K., Vasudaven, D., and Revikumar, K. 2007. "Herbalism: A Prenomenon of New Age in Medicine." *The Internet Journal of Pharmacology* 6, p. 1. Available from: https://ispub.com/IJPHARM/6/1/7976#.
14. Campbell, T. C. and Campbell, T. M. 2006. *The China Study.* Dallas, TX: Benbella Books.
15. Pollan, M. 2008. *In Defense of Food: An Eater's Manifesto.* New York, NY: Penguin Press.
16. Hoffman, I. 2003. "Transcending Reductionism in Nutrition Research." *The American Journal of Clinical Nutrition* 78(3), pp. 5145–5165.
17. Campbell, T. 2010. *Whole: Rethinking the Science of Nutrition.* Dallas, TX: Benbella Books.
18. Nhát, H. and Cheung, L. W. Y. (2010). *Savor: Mindful Eating, Mindful Life.* 1st ed. New York, NY: HarperOne.
19. Dietary Guidelines Advisory Committee (DGAC). Dietary Guidelines for Americans, 2015. Health.gov; Available from: http://www.health.gov/dietaryguidelines/2015.asp.
20. Food Democracy Now! (2014). "About." Available from: http://www.fooddemocracynow.org/about.

MINDFUL EATING REFLECTION JOURNAL

1. Acknowledge
Describe your experience; what did you choose to eat?

2. Intentional Attention

Describe what you noticed during your mindful eating practice.

BREATH:
BODY:
EMOTIONS:
THOUGHTS:
SENSES:

3. Accept Without Judgment
Describe judgment; acceptance

4. Choose Your Experience
Intention/willingness; new perspective

5. Mindful Meditation/Mindful Eating Experience (Mindful Practice)
What did you notice about your meditation experience this week?

MINDFUL EATING WEEKLY QUIZ

This is a brief snapshot of your mindful eating skills. It is to help you to identify which skills you may want to change or enhance. Circle the best answer. Don't forget to notice what you already do well. After you complete this quiz, write down a mindful eating goal for the week.

Take this quiz each week of the course.

1. I tend to stop eating when I am full				
All of the time	Most of the time	Occasionally	Sometimes	Almost Never
2. I eat when I am hungry rather than when I feel emotional				
All of the time	Most of the time	Occasionally	Sometimes	Almost Never
3. I try not to "pick" at food				
All of the time	Most of the time	Occasionally	Sometimes	Almost Never
4. I taste each bite before reaching for the next				
All of the time	Most of the time	Occasionally	Sometimes	Almost Never
5. When I eat, I think about how nourishing the food is for my body				
All of the time	Most of the time	Occasionally	Sometimes	Almost Never
6. I am nonjudgmental of myself, my body and when I accidentally overeat				
All of the time	Most of the time	Occasionally	Sometimes	Almost Never
7. I don't multitask while I eat. When I eat, I just eat and focus on the food in front of me				
All of the time	Most of the time	Occasionally	Sometimes	Almost Never
8. I don't have to eat everything on my plate, I can leave what I don't want				
All of the time	Most of the time	Occasionally	Sometimes	Almost Never
9. I tend to eat slowly, chewing each bite				
All of the time	Most of the time	Occasionally	Sometimes	Almost Never
10. I recognize when I slip into mindless eating (zoned out, popping food into my mouth)				
All of the time	Most of the time	Occasionally	Sometimes	Almost Never

List your Mindful Eating Goals: (ex: learn to be more present when I eat, slow down, stop when I'm full)

Food Energetic Systems

Courtesy of Maria Napoli

I choose food that is alive
With nourishment
Cells bursting with energy
I am in balance
Mindful of satisfying my body
(Napoli)

Food is energy. Learning how to use its effects to support health is an age-old practice (1). From the origins of mankind, hunter-gatherers learned about local plants, and knew which were edible and how to use others in medicinal ways. This type of knowledge of plants and their energetic and medicinal properties formed the basis of Western herbal traditions and traditional Asian medical systems (2). The way we think about food now is very different! We seldom think of food as anything other than containing certain amounts of protein, carbohydrate, fat, minerals, and vitamins. We break apart food in laboratories, analyzing the separate ingredients in an attempt to understand how food helps or harms. Thinking about the nutritional value of food, we "sum total" all of its chemical ingredients before they enter the body.

MAN AS MACHINE

Viewing food in this fashion is defined as "mechanistic" (3). This understanding of food is based on Western scientific beliefs that suggest if we can break down food to its fundamental components we can recreate food out of its basic building blocks. Then, food becomes something that can be made in a laboratory. Synthetically made food is part of our diets whenever we eat processed foods, which are packaged and enhanced with chemicals and flavorings for taste, appearance, shelf life, and efficiency reasons. In response to the negative environmental impact of factory farmed beef, which you'll read more about in Chapter 7, scientists are concocting ways to create beef from the stem cells of cows (4).

This Western view, based on chemistry, may contribute to what nutritionists call food disconnection (5). We eat "food-like" substances, purchased from supermarkets, with no knowledge of where or how it was grown.

VLADGRIN/Shutterstock.com

Stem Cell Food

Simon Booth/Shutterstock.com

If we think instead that food is medicine, and its energy is both nourishing and healing, it fundamentally changes our relationship to nourishment in ways that promote health. How is food a powerful medicine? It is energy and information. Every molecule in our bodies is created from the food we eat, the water we drink, the air we breathe, we literally are what we eat. In choosing to eat whole fresh foods, foods in their natural unrefined forms, we ensure that we consume all of the nutritional needs our bodies require while creating a sense of balance and health. This is because whole grains, beans, nuts, seeds, vegetables, and fruits provide thousands of important phytochemicals that work with our bodies to build and maintain optimal health (6). Beyond the nutritional benefits of a whole-food diet, the energetic properties of food contribute to our well-being and absence of disease. Let's look at two ancient systems of food as medicine with fundamental philosophies of food energetics to better understand the potential benefits from connecting to our food.

TRADITIONAL CHINESE MEDICINE: ANCIENT PRESCRIPTION WITH MODERN BENEFITS

In Chinese medicine, food is seen through the lens of five energies, their capacity to generate sensations of either hot or cold in the human body. The five energy types are cold, hot, warm, cool, and neutral, which refers not only to the state of the food but also its effect on the body (7). Hot tea is one example. Its cool energy means that when we drink hot tea, it generates coolness. In Chinese medicine this means it is a cool beverage. Shortly after drinking hot tea, heat fades quickly and begins to generate cool energy internally, which allows the body to cool off.

In addition to the five energies, Chinese medicine views a balanced diet with the appropriate balance of yin and yang. Yin foods have energetic properties of darkness, slower moving, and colder. Yang foods are the opposite—hotter, faster, and much more energetic. Yin foods are cool and cold; yang foods are hot and warm; and balanced yin and yang are neutral. Here are some examples of different foods and their energies:

	Energy Generated	Examples
Yin	Cold	Tomato, watermelon, banana, grapefruit, seaweed, kelp, sprouts, lettuces, salt, soy sauce
Yin	Cool	Millet, barley, wheat, buckwheat, eggplant, cucumber, celery, peppermint, broccoli, spinach, apple, egg whites, sesame oil, cream, yogurt and cheese
Balanced yin and yang	Neutral	Rice, corn, sweet potato, carrot, cabbage, black sesame, sunflower seed, plums, grapes, lemon, mushrooms, shrimp, pork, beef, egg yolk, honey, milk, soymilk, sugar
Yang	Warm	Onion, leeks, green onion, sweet peppers, spearmint, peach, raspberry, pumpkin, walnut, seafood, garlic, ginger, nutmeg, rosemary, coffee, wine, vegetable oil, chicken, ham, goat milk, brown sugar
Yang	Hot	Black pepper, cinnamon, chili pepper, mustard seed

In addition to the energetic qualities attributed to foods by Chinese medicine practitioners, there are five predominant tastes: pungent, sweet, sour, bitter, and salty. Each taste corresponds with a different organ system, and a balanced approach to diet is important to fully support the entire body. For example, pungent tastes are believed to support the lungs and the large intestines, and sweet tastes support the stomach and the spleen. The Chinese believe both flavor and the energetics of yin and yang must both be considered in order to fully support health, or recovery from illness.

What then is the Chinese medicine prescription for nutritional health? To maintain health, one must consume the right balance of yin, yang, and neutral foods. In the Eastern traditions, herbs are considered food and help support the digestive processes of the body (8). Herbs can help to balance the qualities of yin and yang present in all foods. Each food has a combination of yin and yang elements that are complimentary, existing in food in a dynamic way that balances its energetic properties. Using herbs in ways that supplement the underlying energetic properties of foods can be a helpful adjunct therapy that leads to a balanced energetic approach to the foods we consume.

4 Step MAC Guide

Mindful Eating Exercise: Discovering the Five Tastes

The skill of eating mindfully allows us to slow down and savor our food. As we turn inward, we notice the entire flavor palate of food, even different tastes. This mindful eating exercise helps us find the five tastes: pungent, sweet, sour, bitter, and salty.

Find a place to eat your next meal with few distractions. Perhaps, a quiet place where you can fully focus on the experience of eating.

CHOOSE your first bite. Focus on this bite with clarity and focus. Notice the entire experience of the bite: the colors, texture, and shapes. Choose a "bite-sized" portion that can fit into your mouth easily. Just the right amount.

TASTE your second bite. Can you find the five tastes? What is pungent? Some examples are garlic or chili peppers. Is it sweet, like the freshest peach? Sour might taste like a lemon, or even yogurt. Is bitter tastes are found in some spices, or dark leafy greens such as kale or arugula. Salty tastes are found in sea vegetables, miso, or table salt. See if you can find the full notes of the flavors in your bite.

NOTICE your third bite with curiosity, as if you are a scientist. Feel the food as it moves in your mouth and down your throat. Can you sense it move into your stomach? If you notice any feelings, are they anxiety or fear? Or is it just hunger? Pace yourself with intention, and put your fork or spoon down, taking five breaths. Continue to notice your feelings.

RELAX THE GRIP: Before the fourth bite, add a brief pause. Instead of taking the bite without interruption, just stop for a brief moment then bring the bite to your mouth. As you chew, take a brief break. Continue this pattern adding a little pause for the bites that follow. This relaxes the "grip" of eating that can propel us from bite to bite without noticing our levels of hunger.

A mindful eater knows that only through practice, curiosity, and gentleness can the skill of mindful eating (and mindfulness in general) be learned.

Take a moment to journal about your experiences from this exercise.

_____

_____

_____

_____

_____

_____

_____

_____

_____

_____

AYURVEDA: A RECIPE FOR HEALTHY LIVING

Ayurveda (pronounced i-yer-vay-da) is an ancient system of holistic healthcare that is becoming increasingly popular in the West today. Ayurvedic medicine focuses on all areas of health, including diet, lifestyle, exercise, detoxification, sleep, and the mind.

A sister science to Yoga, Ayurveda emerged from the sacred texts of ancient India, known as the *Vedas,* or "Books of Wisdom." These date back at least 5,000 years and are widely regarded as humanity's oldest literature (9). As a completely universal body of wisdom, Ayurvedic practices are as relevant today as they were 5,000 years ago. Ayurvedic principles can be woven into any culture or time period, because they are rooted in the laws and cycles of Mother Nature.

According to Ayurveda, health is not a *state* defined by lab tests or yearly check-ups. Health is a continuous and participatory *process* that embraces all aspects of life: physical, mental, emotional, behavioral, spiritual, familial, social, and universal. Achieving balance on all levels of being is the true measure of vibrant health. The average person and standardized treatment simply do not exist in Ayurvedic medicine. Every individual is a one-of-a-kind with an equally unique blueprint for health. By providing a universal framework for understanding these blueprints, Ayurveda teaches us to honor and support our true individual natures.

The underlying prescription of Ayurvedic medicine is quite simple: recognize the power of self-healing within, and you will become your own greatest doctor (10).

In the Ayurvedic system, the individual mind–body or psychophysiological constitution is called one's dosha (11). The tridosha system offers a simple and complete way to understand how the foods we eat affect our body's energies.

Ayurveda is literally the "science of life", or of longevity. Nearly 3,000 years ago, Ayurvedic practitioners approached health and healing as a practice that balanced the five basic elements of the cosmos: earth, air, fire, water, and space. In human beings, these five elements occur in the form of the three *doshas,* forces that along with the seven (dhatus) tissues and three malas (waste products) make up the human body.

The Three Doshas. When in balance, the three doshas maintain health, and when an imbalance occurs among them, they cause the normal functioning of the body to go out of balance leading to disease. Imbalances indicate an increase or decrease in one, two, or all three of the doshas. The three doshas are vata (air), pitta (fire), and kapha (water/earth). According to the Ayurvedic system, we each have all three doshas present, with one most dominant. When out of balance, we can suffer from disturbance; meaning one or more of the doshas is out of balance. Vata dosha is made up of the elements of air and space. It is viewed energetically as kinetic energy, and is responsible for all body movement and nervous functions. Vata is found below the navel and in the organs below, as well as the nervous system, pelvic region, thighs, and legs. Its disruption is manifested as gas and muscular or nervous energy, leading to pain.

Pitta is made up of the element of fire. It governs all enzymes in the body and hormones and is responsible for digestion, pigmentation, body temperature, hunger, thirst, sight, courage, and mental activity. Pitta is located between the navel and the chest (going upward from the navel, where vata is downward), it is in the stomach, small intestines, liver, spleen, skin, and blood; its principal "seat" is in the stomach. When disrupted, or disturbed, its manifestation is acid, which leads to inflammation.

Kapha is made up of the elements of earth and water. It represents the principle of stability and cohesion. Kapha's job is to regulate pitta and vata energies, and is responsible for keeping the body lubricated and maintaining its solid nature and strength, as well as vitality. It is located in the upper part of the body and the upper portion of the stomach, fat tissues, and areas between joints; its principal seat is in the lungs. When disrupted, kapha disturbance manifests as mucus and liquid leading to swelling.

Vata's qualities are dryness, cold, light, irregularity, mobility, roughness, and abundance. These qualities emerge in contrast to the attributes of vata. For example, the vata energetic attribute of motion can lead to the side effect of dryness. Too much dryness produces irregularity of body and mind. Pitta is hot, light, intense, fluid, liquid, putrid, pungent, and sour. Heat appears when pitta is disturbed and results from change caused by pitta. The intensity of excessive heat produces irritability in the body and mind. Kapha is heavy, cold, stable, dense, soft, and smooth. When disturbed, heaviness occurs and results from firmness caused by kapha. This produces slowness in the body and mind.

All diseases or ills are viewed as disruptions in the balance of the three doshas. The seven "normal" doshic body constitutions are vata, pitta, kapha, vata-pitta, pitta-kapha, vata-kapha, and sama. Sama is triple balanced, and is extremely rare. Most of us are a combination of doshas with one type predominant. In general, vata type people are light and "airy" with energetic imbalances that include anxiety and fearfulness. Pitta types, with their fiery qualities, are aggressive and impatient, exhibiting fiery and hot headed characteristics, and are prone to pitta type diseases. Kapha types are stable and entrenched, solid, and dependable; they exhibit heavy, wet, and earthy characteristics, and are prone to kapha diseases.

Rasa (Taste by the Tongue)	Element	Doshic Effect
Sweet	Earth and water	kapha, pitta, & vata
Sour	Earth and fire	kapha & pitta, vata
Saline	Water and fire	kapha & pitta, vata
Pungent	Wind and fire	pitta & vata, kapha
Bitter	Wind and space	vata, pitta & kapha
Astringent	Wind and earth	vata, kapha & pitta

Herbal medicine and the kitchen treat disease in the Ayurvedic system. Foods and drugs are classified by the tongue, potency, and taste after digestion.

> Here is a quiz to help you determine what dosha you are. If you were to see an Ayurvedic physician you would most likely begin your visit by taking a quiz just like this one.

Dosha Quiz: What Type Are You?

Take the following quiz to determine your dosha type. Circle the best answer.

Body Structure			
	Vata	Pitta	Kapha
Face	Oblong or narrow	Angular with strong features	Round with soft features
Eyes	Small	Deep set, medium	Large
Nose Bridge	Narrow width to the bridge	Medium width to the bridge	Wider and flatter
Lips	Thin	Medium	Full
Complexion	Lack luster or a dusty gray	Rosy, ruddy	Pale
Hair	Coarse fibers but scanty and dry	Fine fiber, oily, may experience early gray	Coarse fibers, oily, and quite full or dense

Body Structure			
	Vata	Pitta	Kapha
Skin	The skin is thin	The skin has a medium thickness	The skin is thick
Bones	The length to width ratio makes the bone appear narrow.	The length to width ratio is moderate	The length to width ratio makes the bones stocky or stout
Neck	Long	Medium	Short
Hand	Rectangular palm with narrow fingers	Square palm with medium fingers	Square, fleshy palm with short or stout fingers
Fingernails	Thin and may be fragile	Medium and stronger	Thick and strongest
Weight/Body fat	Light or has frequent ups and downs	Moderate and relatively steady with a slow gain during the midlife years	Tends to be consistently heavily and stocky throughout life
Musculature	Minimal	Moderate, strong, and reasonably well defined	Bulky, stocky
Body build	Ectomorph	Mesomorph	Endomorph
Chart totals			

Body Function			
	Vata	Pitta	Kapha
Appetite	Picky, variable, sometimes forgets to eat, and little things can cause you to lose your appetite	Consistently strong and not easily lost	Consistently low
Digestion	Gas and bloating occur frequently. Gas has little odor	Burning indigestion or smelly gas are common challenges	Feels heavy after meals. Food does not seem to digest for a long time
Elimination	Stools are hard. There is straining. Sometime skips days	Softer and sometimes loose. Elimination occurs 1–3 times per day	Stools occur only once per day, they are almost always solid and log like. If out of balance, there may be mucous in the stool
Sweat	Does not sweat easily	Sweats easily and has stronger body odor	Sweats easily with exercise. There is pleasant body odor

(Continued)

Body Function			
	Vata	Pitta	Kapha
Body temperature	Feels cold easily and enjoys the heat	Often feels warm and enjoys cool temperatures	Does not feel too warm or too cold too often
Skin	Skin is dry and rough. Lips may crack	Skin is oily with a tendency to develop red rashes or acne	Skin is soft and moist. If problems develop, they are moist or oily
Menses	The cycle is often irregular and painful. Bleeding is light and lasts 2–4 days	The cycle is regular, and the flow is heavy for 3–5 days	The cycle is regular, flow is moderate and lasts for 5–7 days
Sleep	Sleep is light and easily disturbed. There may be frequent periods of insomnia	Falls asleep easily and sleeps well most of the time unless it is too hot	Falls asleep easily and sleeps deeply. Rarely wakes up from noises and may be hard to awaken
Chart Totals			
Total (Structure and Function Combined)			

Knowing Your Dosha: Why It Matters

Dr. David Frawley is known as a leading authority on Ayurveda and Yoga. He has written over 20 books over the past 20 years, including *Yoga & Ayurveda: Self-Healing and Self-Realization* (7). In this seminal work on Ayurveda, he reminds us that Yoga and Ayurveda form a complete approach for optimal health, vitality, and higher awareness. Reminding us that the secret powers of the body, breath, senses, mind, and even chakras can be healing, our understanding of Ancient Wisdom can shed light on what ails us and reconnect us to our essential selves. Yoga and Ayurveda is considered timeless wisdom and its relevance for us may help us heal in more holistic ways. In the West, we think of Yoga as a purely physical practice of asana, with classes everywhere. But its broadness and more spiritual essential nature have helped millions heal over thousands of years.

Ayurveda may play a similar role in our lives. As a special system of natural medicine, Ayurveda's acceptance in the West may lead to alternative approaches to mend physical and mental diseases caused in part by disconnection to our essential selves. Those who have learned how yoga can help heal the physical body should remember that the intention is not to use it alone; rather, yoga and its physical practices are designed for use in an Ayurvedic context. The combined study of yoga and Ayurveda is important for helping learn and understand the whole of life and promote an integration of body, mind and spirit—what we all seek.

An Ayurvedic Recipe for Health

Mung beans are small green legumes that have been a part of Ayurvedic cuisine for thousands of years. Sprouted, we know them as bean sprouts. As a plant-based food, there are many reasons why these special little green beans should enjoy a role in your diet. They can be eaten either raw or cooked, you can add their sprouts to just about anything, and you can easily grow them yourself. Since they are slightly sweet in flavor, try throwing them into your desserts. This is already the case in some Asian countries, where mung bean paste is used to make frozen desserts.

In Ayurveda, mung beans are considered extremely easy to digest and are considered purifying and cleansing. Mung beans pack a nice nutritional punch—they are high in potassium, fiber, magnesium, and B vitamins, and they are also a good source of vitamin C. Try using these little beans in your own plant-based cooking. Enjoy this easy recipe and its wonderful combination of cleansing fresh herbs and purifying beans.

Marina Shanti/Shutterstock.com

Basil Mung Bean Salad (Author's Recipe)

Yield: Makes ~ 4 servings

Ingredients

1 cup mung beans, cooked according to directions on bag

5 cups diced or thinly sliced cabbage and carrots

1 large handful fresh basil (about a cup), coarsely chopped

1 tablespoon olive oil

1 avocado, sliced

To taste: sea salt

Directions

In a large skillet, heat the olive oil on medium low. Add the carrots and cabbage, and sauté about 3 minutes.

Add the mung beans, and continue to sauté, stirring occasionally, until the cabbage is translucent, about 5 minutes.

Add sea salt to taste.

Stir in the basil and saute another minute.

Take off the stove and add in the sliced avocado.

REFERENCES

1. Schmidt, L. 2014. "Sustainable Living and Conscious Eating." In *Beyond Stress: Strategies for Blissful Living*, ed., Napoli, M. Dubuque, IA: Kendall Hunt Press.
2. Clarke, P. 2008. "Aboriginal Healing Practices and Australian Bush Medicine." *Journal of the Anthropological Society of South Australia* 33, pp. 3–33.
3. Leggett, D. 2012. "The Energetics of Food—The Language of Food Energetics." *Qi Nutrition*. Available from: http://www.meridianpress.net/articles/energetics-of-food-4.html.
4. Woollaston and Reilly. 2013. "At Least It Tastes of Meat!: World's First Test-Tube Artificial Beef 'Googleburger' Gets GOOD Review as It's Eaten for the First Time." *Daily Mail UK*. Available from: http://www.dailymail.co.uk/sciencetech/article-2384715/At-tastes-meat--Worlds-test-tube-artificial-beef-Googleburger-gets-GOOD-review-eaten-time.html.

5. McWilliams, J. 2011. "Connecting with Our Food, Disconnecting with Ourselves." *James McWilliams*. Available from: http://james-mcwilliams.com/?p=305.
6. Segersten, A. and Malterre, T. 2007. *The Whole Life Nutrition Cookbook: Whole Foods Recipes for Personal and Planetary Health*. Bellingham, WA: Whole Life Press.
7. Frawley, D. 1999. *Yoga & Ayurveda: Self-Healing and Self-Realization*. Twin Lakes, WI: Lotus Press.
8. Cousins, G. 2000. *Conscious Eating*. Berkeley, CA: North Atlantic Books..
9. Yarema, T., Rhoda, D., and Brannigan, J. 2014. *Eat, Taste, Heal: An Ayurvedic Guidebook and Cookbook for Modern Living*. Kapaii, HI: Five Elements Press.
10. Frawley, D. 2000. *Ayurvedic Healing*. 2nd ed. Twin Lakes, WI: Lotus Press.
11. Zysk, K. 2011. "Traditional Medicine of India: Ayurveda and Siddha." In *Fundamentals of Complementary and Alternative Medicine*, 4th edition. ed., Micozzi, M. St. Louis, MI: Elsevier, pp. 455–467.

Mindful Eating Reflection Journal

1. Acknowledge
Describe your experience; what did you choose to eat?

2. Intentional Attention

Describe what you noticed during your mindful eating practice.

BREATH:	
BODY:	
EMOTIONS:	
THOUGHTS:	
SENSES:	

3. Accept Without Judgment
Describe judgment; acceptance

4. Choose Your Experience
Intention/willingness; new perspective

5. Mindful Meditation/Mindful Eating Experience (Mindful Practice)
What did you notice about your meditation experience this week?

MINDFUL EATING WEEKLY QUIZ

This is a brief snapshot of your mindful eating skills. It is to help you to identify which skills you may want to change or enhance. Circle the best answer. Don't forget to notice what you already do well. After you complete this quiz, write down a mindful eating goal for the week.

Take this quiz each week of the course.

1. I tend to stop eating when I am full				
All of the time	Most of the time	Occasionally	Sometimes	Almost Never
2. I eat when I am hungry rather than when I feel emotional				
All of the time	Most of the time	Occasionally	Sometimes	Almost Never
3. I try not to "pick" at food				
All of the time	Most of the time	Occasionally	Sometimes	Almost Never
4. I taste each bite before reaching for the next				
All of the time	Most of the time	Occasionally	Sometimes	Almost Never
5. When I eat, I think about how nourishing the food is for my body				
All of the time	Most of the time	Occasionally	Sometimes	Almost Never
6. I am nonjudgmental of myself, my body and when I accidentally overeat				
All of the time	Most of the time	Occasionally	Sometimes	Almost Never
7. I don't multitask while I eat. When I eat, I just eat and focus on the food in front of me				
All of the time	Most of the time	Occasionally	Sometimes	Almost Never
8. I don't have to eat everything on my plate, I can leave what I don't want				
All of the time	Most of the time	Occasionally	Sometimes	Almost Never
9. I tend to eat slowly, chewing each bite				
All of the time	Most of the time	Occasionally	Sometimes	Almost Never
10. I recognize when I slip into mindless eating (zoned out, popping food into my mouth)				
All of the time	Most of the time	Occasionally	Sometimes	Almost Never

List your Mindful Eating Goals: (ex: learn to be more present when I eat, slow down, stop when I'm full)

Courtesy of Maria Napoli

The battle between my brain and desire
Continue to challenge each other
I will strive to eat only when hungry
Allow myself to say no to foods that do not serve me
Know that when I indulge in eating treats they are just that "treats"
The battle is over as I make conscious decisions
My brain and desire are in balance

(Napoli)

Eating is personal. We choose food for many reasons; cultural practices, habits, connection to our family traditions, comfort, ease, health, and taste preferences are some of the reasons. At the same time, we struggle in America with conditions related to eating too much food, what scientists call over nourishment. In other parts of the world, people are starving. In our land of plenty there are ample opportunities to eat anything, at any time of year, whatever we desire, independent of growing season, climate, or proximity. All our desires can be satisfied by a trip to the supermarket or fast food outlet, whenever we want.

This chapter is a story of the brain, and how our moods are affected by certain food choices. We are just beginning to understand its complexity and how we may affect different mood states based on many things, including food choices. Remember as you read through this chapter that there is no judgment intended about the choices you make; rather, the journey is about noticing how you feel in the present moment without judgment. In this fashion, we know there is no "good" food or "bad" food, but simply food. Different foods have different consequences. Let's learn more about the food and mood connection now.

Olga Zelenskaya/Shutterstock.com

Is satisfying hunger the same as eating for the sake of indulging in delicious foods? When we eat a meal, we become calmer, and more lethargic. We share this in common with any other animal. Hunger has the opposite effect—we become irritable, alert, and often short tempered. In biological terms, the drive to find food is part of the evolutionary goal to stay alive. When feeling out of sorts, especially irritable, we are driven to seek a feeding opportunity that leads to the biological rest and digest response, part of the parasympathetic nervous system. This relationship, eating is good; not eating is bad, is only one part of the complicated and complex relationship we have with food, our brain, and our moods.

This primal reaction to hunger and feeding is more complex than it appears. The details of the relationship between food and mood end up being a little confusing and a lot complicated. Humans eat for many different reasons, under a variety of different circumstances. Some are connected with our emotions, and others are less clear. However, looking at why we eat and the effect on our brain framed against the modern backdrop of ever present quantities of all types of foods, constant stimulation to eat driven by advertising and abundance, and manipulations of taste by savvy food marketers, can begin to shed light on the nuanced and messy relationship we have with biology, choice, and overeating.

WHY DO WE EAT?

In simplest terms, we eat to stay alive. In Chapter 2, we discussed the energetics of food in a holistic and integrated way. Let's look at the science of assimilation. Assimilation is the dynamic interaction of the forces of food with the forces of our human bodies. Humans convert the energy from plants and animals into our own cellular fuel. Using cellular respiration, the body releases energy that is used to produce energy molecules. Cellular respiration is the process in which our bodies' cells produce the energy they need to survive. In cellular respiration, cells use oxygen to break down the sugar **glucose** and store its energy in molecules of adenosine triphosphate (ATP). Cellular respiration is critical for the survival of most living things because the energy in glucose cannot be used by cells until it is stored in ATP. Cells use ATP to power virtually all of their activities—to grow, divide, replace worn out cell parts, and execute many other tasks. Cellular respiration provides the energy required for an amoeba to glide toward food, the Venus fly trap to capture its prey, or the ballet dancer to execute stunning leaps. Cellular respiration occurs within a cell constantly, day and night, and if it ceases, the cell—and ultimately the organism—dies (1).

Two critical ingredients required for cellular respiration are glucose and oxygen. The glucose used in cellular respiration enters cells in a variety of ways. Plants, algae, and certain bacteria make their own glucose through photosynthesis, the process by which plants use light to convert carbon dioxide and water into sugar. Animals (including humans) obtain glucose by eating plants and other animals, and fungi and bacteria absorb glucose as they break down the tissues of plants and animals. Regardless of how they obtain it, cells must have a steady supply of glucose so that ATP production is continuous.

Oxygen is present in the air, and is also found dissolved in water. It either diffuses into cells—as in bacteria, fungi, plants, and many aquatic animals, such as sponges and fish—or it is inhaled—as in more complex animals, including humans. Cellular respiration, sometimes, is referred to as aerobic respiration, meaning that it occurs in the presence of oxygen.

Cellular respiration transfers about 40% of the energy of glucose to ATP. The rest of the energy from glucose is released as heat, which warm-blooded organisms use to maintain body temperature, and cold-blooded organisms release to the atmosphere. Cellular respiration is strikingly efficient compared to other energy conversion processes, such as the burning of gasoline, in which only about 25% of the energy is used and about 75% is released as heat (1).

When we eat a meal, nutrients are released from food through digestion. Digestion begins in the mouth by the action of chewing and the chemical activity of saliva, a watery fluid that contains enzymes, certain proteins that help break down food. Further digestion occurs as food travels through the stomach and the small intestine, where digestive enzymes and acids liquefy food and muscle contractions push it along the digestive tract. Large food molecules, such as fats, carbohydrates, and proteins, are broken apart releasing glucose and other nutrients. This released energy is then used in many ways, including the buildup of other large molecules. One example of a large molecule the body needs to build are proteins which make up the body's structure, and temporary energy storage "places" such as fat and glycogen.

Nutrients are absorbed from the inside of the small intestine into the bloodstream and carried to the sites in the body where they are needed. At these sites, several chemical reactions occur that ensure the growth and function of body tissues. The parts of foods that are not absorbed continue to move down the intestinal tract and are eliminated from the body as feces (2).

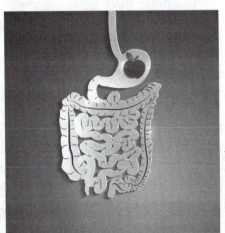

Once digested, carbohydrates, proteins, and fats provide the body with the energy it needs to maintain its several functions. Scientists measure this energy in kilocalories, the amount of energy needed to raise 1 kilogram of water to 1 degree Celsius. In nutrition discussions, scientists use the term calorie instead of kilocalorie as the standard unit of measure in nutrition.

The drive to eat is biologically based (3). Mood regulation is also biologically based, with feeding leading to ease, and hunger leading to restlessness and discomfort (4). Sounds simple. The ancient practices of Ayurveda and Chinese Medicine understand this model of the body and our innate self-regulatory mechanisms of biological drives as part of the process for diagnosing diseases caused by eating too much, too little, or by eating food in the wrong combinations. However, in modern times, we suffer from diseases related to overeating such as obesity, diabetes, irritable bowel syndrome, and heart disease. Experts believe all are related to eating too much food or the wrong *types* of foods including those that are highly processed. In addition, research now focuses on how eating certain foods affect our brain, leading to difficult moods including anxiety and depression (5).

We now wonder what comes first, the chicken or the egg? Do our food choices affect our moods, or do our moods lead to the "wrong" choices of food?

In a recent study (6), researchers considered this question and looked at food choice and moods. In a summary of the existing research (what is referred to as a "meta-analysis"), they found a connection between negative emotions and choosing unhealthy foods. When we are in a bad mood, we tend to reach for highly processed sugary treats such as cookies, candy, and snacks. The researchers also wondered if there was any connection to food choice and positive moods. When they surveyed the literature, there were mixed findings, so the study authors attempted to test their hypothesis: if they injected the element of time into the scientific equation, would that change the relationship between food and mood? What they found was regardless of mood, *long-term, future focused thinking* led to healthier food choices.

Their finding suggests that being in a good mood helps us take a longer-term perspective. But does choosing healthier foods, such as fresh fruits and vegetables, lean protein, whole grains, and drinking plenty of water, lead to a sustained good mood? Conversely, if we eat what we might describe as comfort food, which nutritionally might mean primarily carbohydrate and fat-laden cookies, cakes, chips, crackers, and other processed snack foods, does this put us in a bad mood? And finally, how does our brain regulate how much we eat?

Before we answer that question, let's go back to the brain and the biological response. For thousands of years, human food consumption was regulated through a complex hormone response that was designed to get us to find food and eat when hungry, and stop eating when satisfied. In addition to

the hormones involved in the stress response (which cause us to seek out and find food), there are hormones that regulate our digestive response, signaling that it's time to stop eating and focus on digestion. The brain, through the HPA Axis, controls these responses. Scientists believe we rely on a remarkable, naturally occurring hormone called leptin to regulate what we eat, and it also tells our brain when we've had enough. However, it appears that leptin's ability to regulate appetite has gone awry, leading to overeating and obesity. But why are we eating more?

It is suggested that leptin's signals to the brain are not being "heard" (7). The hormone leptin, which comes from the Greek *leptos*, meaning thin, has a role in energy balance and metabolism. Leptin is secreted by fat cells, and when working properly, your body responds to leptin by signaling the brain to decrease your appetite after you've eaten. Leptin also promotes calorie burning. It was discovered by accident in the mid-1990s when researchers found that mice treated with leptin ate considerably less, and mice with less leptin overate. It works the same way in people, with a twist: obese people have high levels of leptin, but researchers at Harvard and elsewhere think their bodies are less sensitive to its effects. Leptin resistance, as it's known, results in "unnecessarily high food intake," and low leptin levels are a precursor to obesity (7–10).

So why then, if the body has an innate system, honed by eons of trial and error to regulate fat stores and keep the body in homeostasis, is the United States and many other countries facing an obesity epidemic of unprecedented scale? What causes leptin resistance? Research shows a connection to overexposure to high levels of leptin hormone, caused by eating too much sugar (11).

Scientists have known about this process ("resistance") occurring with the hormone insulin. Insulin regulates how the body uses and stores glucose and fat. High blood sugar levels cause repeated surges in insulin, and this causes the body's cells to become "insulin-resistant", which leads to the production of even higher levels of insulin, eventually leading to type 2 diabetes (12). It is much the same as being in a room with a strong odor for a period of time. Eventually, you stop being able to smell it, because the signal no longer gets through. The same process also occurs with leptin. It has been shown that as sugar gets metabolized and stored as triglycerides in fat cells, the fat cells release surges of leptin, and those surges result in leptin-resistance, just as it results in insulin-resistance. When you become leptin-resistant, the body can no longer hear the messages telling it to stop eating and burn fat–so it remains hungry and stores more fat.

Everett Collection/Shutterstock.com

This will not only contribute to weight gain, but also increase the risk of many chronic illnesses, as leptin plays a significant, if not primary, role in heart disease, obesity, diabetes, osteoporosis, autoimmune diseases, reproductive disorders, and perhaps, the rate of aging itself (13).

The science of leptin research is producing astounding findings. Researchers in 2013 studied the relationship between diet, body weight, and leptin regulation (9). Observing that chronic consumption of a Western-type diet, containing both high levels of sugar and fat results in leptin resistance, they hypothesized that fructose, as part of the sugar component of Western-type diets, is one cause ingredient in the development of leptin resistance. In their research, they speculated that if they removed fructose they would then prevent leptin resistance even if subjects (rats) ate a high fat diet. They fed study rats a sugar-free high fat diet or a high-fructose high fat diet for 134 days. The high-fructose diet resulted in impaired responses to leptin. They saw that the rats who were on a sugar free, high-fat diet had no problem with leptin response. They then switched the groups, and showed the opposite effect—rats that were completely responsive to leptin and body weight regulation when on a sugar-free high fat diet lost their regulatory ability, and became leptin resistant (and gained weight). The other rats, which had previously been leptin resistant, regained their ability to regulate their weight when they got off fructose and went on a sugar-free high fat diet. The study authors concluded that a diet containing both fructose and fat (which is very much like the standard American diet) leads to leptin resistance, while a sugar-free high fat diet does not. Especially important is that *removing* fructose from the diet reversed the leptin resistance (9).

We'll read more about sugar in the next chapter, but the implications are chilling. It appears that our Western high sugar, high fat mostly processed food Standard American Diet (SAD) diet is to blame for its impact on elevated body weight. So we can conclude that the brain is responsible for weight gain, with leptin being the hormone that's not properly "heard" by the brain. But back to the brain and mood regulation—is a highly processed food diet responsible for mental health disturbances such as anxiety and depression? In other words, does our food affect our mood?

For thousands of years, people have believed that food could influence their health and well-being. During the Middle Ages, people started to take great interest in how certain foods affected their mood and temperament. Many medical culinary textbooks of the time described the relationship between food and mood. For example, quince, dates, and elderberries were used as mood enhancers, lettuce and chicory as tranquilizers, and apples, pomegranates, beef, and eggs as erotic stimulants (14). The past

80 years has seen immense progress in research, primarily short-term human trials and animal studies, showing how certain foods alter brain structure, chemistry, and physiology. This affects mood and performance. These studies suggest that foods directly influencing brain neurotransmitter systems have the greatest effects on mood. In turn, mood can also influence our food choices, and *expectations* on the effects of certain foods can influence our perception.

The Complex Mood–Food Relationships: Why It Matters

Sunsinger/Shutterstock.com

The relationship between food and mood in individuals is complex and depends "on the time of day, the type and macronutrient composition of food, the amount of food consumed, and the age and dietary history of the subject" (15). Modern scientific nutrition research has demonstrated what Ancient Wisdom held to be true: there is an individual nutritional prescription that "fits" each person, since the complexity of biological interactions is quite individualized. For example, in one study by Spring et al. (16), 184 adults either ate a protein-rich or carbohydrate-rich meal. After 2 hours, their mood and performance were measured (16). The effects of the meal different for female and male subjects and for younger and older participants. For example, females reported greater sleepiness after a carbohydrate meal and males reported greater calmness. In addition, participants aged 40 years or older showed impairments on a test of sustained focused attention after a carbohydrate lunch.

Circadian rhythms also influence energy levels and performance throughout the day. People who describe themselves as "early birds" feel most productive in the first part of the day, and their food choices become particularly important during lunch and throughout the afternoon. Those who are "night owls" feel most energetic later in the day and should pay attention to their breakfast choices as they can increase or decrease energy levels and influence cognitive functioning. These findings were suggested in another research study. Michaud et al. (17) found if you are an evening person and you skip breakfast, your cognitive performance might be impaired. A large breakfast rich in protein could improve your recall performance but might impair your concentration. This illustrates just how complex the relationship between food and mood are. It also suggests that Ancient Wisdom knew best—we must match our own individual patterns with the right food choices to find a healthy balance.

SEROTONIN: THE IMPACT OF CARBOHYDRATES AND PROTEIN

Serotonin is an important neurotransmitter that the brain produces from tryptophan contained in foods such as clams, oysters, escargots, octopus, squids, banana, pineapple, plum, nuts, milk, turkey, spinach, and eggs. Functions of serotonin include the regulation of sleep, appetite, and impulse control. Increased serotonin levels are related to mood elevation. Researchers have considered theories suggesting that a diet rich in carbohydrates can relieve depression and elevate mood in disorders such as carbohydrate craving obesity, pre-menstrual syndrome, and seasonal affective disorder (SAD) (18). They theorized that increased patients' carbohydrate intake associated with these disorders represented self-medicating attempts and that carbohydrates increased serotonin synthesis. A protein rich diet, in contrary, decreases brain serotonin levels.

Controlling the amount of serotonin in the brain is limited by the availability of its precursor tryptophan, an amino acid. The large amino acids such as tryptophan, valine, tyrosine, and leucine share the same transport carrier across the blood–brain barrier. They then compete with each other for the ability to pair up with a transporter to take serotonin into the brain, boosting mood. Eating foods high in protein increases the amount of many amino acids in the blood but not of tryptophan, which is only found in low doses in dietary protein. This means that many large amino acids compete with a small amount of tryptophan for transport into the brain, meaning that less tryptophan is available for serotonin synthesis.

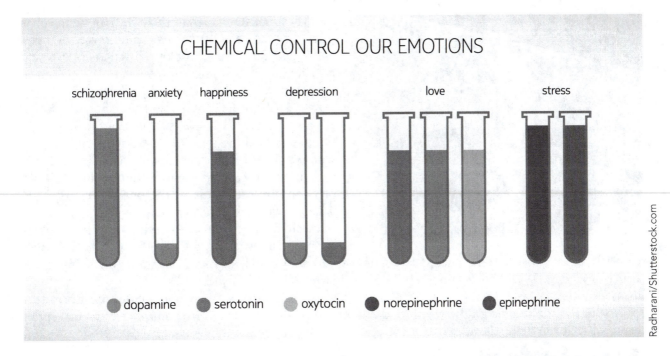

CHEMICAL CONTROL OUR EMOTIONS

schizophrenia   anxiety   happiness   depression   love   stress

● dopamine   ● serotonin   ● oxytocin   ● norepinephrine   ● epinephrine

Radharani/Shutterstock.com

We can theoretically change this through consuming foods high in carbohydrates, which changes amino acid levels in the blood. As blood glucose (sugar) levels rise, insulin is released and enables muscle tissues to take up most amino acids except for tryptophan, which is bound to albumin in the blood. As a result, the ratio of tryptophan relative to other amino acids in the blood increases, which enables tryptophan to bind to transporters, enter the brain in large amounts, and stimulate serotonin synthesis (18).

Radharani/Shutterstock.com

Does this mean that if we're depressed we should eat a lot of carbohydrates? Not so. Benton and Donohoe (18) found that only a protein content of less than 2% of a meal helped raise serotonin levels. Foods high in carbohydrates such as bread and potatoes contain 15% and 10% of calories, respectively, that come from protein thereby undermining the effects of carbohydrates on serotonin levels. This does not mean that "carbohydrate craving" is an explanation for our desire for foods such as chocolate, ice cream, and other sweets. Some think that these cravings are one way to get serotonin levels raised. However, most of their calories come from fat and contain enough protein to undermine any effect of carbohydrates on serotonin levels (19). Cravings for sweets may come from birth, and we'll read more about this in the next chapter.

Omega-3 fatty acids can influence mood, behavior, and personality. Low blood levels of polyunsaturated omega-3 fatty acids which are found in flaxseed oil, walnuts, soybeans, and salmon (as four examples) are associated with depression, pessimism, and impulsivity, according to a study by the University of Pittsburgh Medical Center (20). In addition, they can play a role in major depressive disorder, bipolar disorder, schizophrenia, substance abuse, and attention deficit disorder. In recent decades, people in Western developed countries have consumed greater amounts of omega-6 polyunsaturated fatty acids, contained in foods such as eggs, poultry, baked goods, whole-grain bread, nuts, and many oils, that outcompete omega-3 polyunsaturated fatty acids. Especially docosahexaenoic acid (DHA) and eicosapentaenoic acid (EPA), both members of the omega-3 fatty acid family, contribute to the fluidity of the cell membrane, thereby playing an important role in brain development and functioning. Omega-3 fatty acids are found in fish, other seafood including algae and krill, some plants, meat, and nut oils. Many foods such as bread, yogurt, orange juice, milk, and eggs are oftentimes fortified with omega-3 fatty acids as well.

Courtesy of Maria Napoli

Micronutrients such as thiamine (found in cereal grains, pork, yeast, potatoes, cauliflower, oranges, and eggs) can help boost overall energy levels and lift moods. A deficiency in iron status can result in depressed mood, lethargy, and problems with attention (14). Iron deficiency also results in a decreased ability to exercise. Foods rich in iron include liver, vegetables such as broccoli, asparagus, and parsley, seafood, iron-fortified grains, greens, nuts, meat, and dried fruits. The micronutrient folic acid also plays an important role in the brain. Folic acid deficiency, which is rare in the general population, is associated with depressed mood. Psychiatric patients are particularly at risk for developing folic acid deficiency because of possible disordered eating habits caused by a loss of appetite and anticonvulsant drugs, which inhibit folic acid absorption (19). Foods rich in folic acid include dark, leafy green vegetables, liver and other organ meats, poultry, oranges and grapefruits, nuts, sprouts, and whole wheat breads.

Although the interaction between food and mood is complex, there are a number of dietary interventions that can help relieve anxiety and depression. Recommendations include:

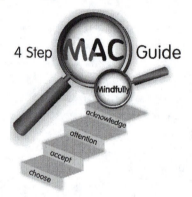

4 Step **MAC** Guide
Mindfully
acknowledge
attention
accept
choose

- Follow a diet plan that prevents hypoglycemia (e.g., eliminate or reduce refined sugar, alcohol, caffeine, and tobacco; eat 4–6 small meals throughout the day; eat plenty of dietary fiber.
- An elimination or rotation diet will help to decide whether or not you have sensitivities to particular foods.

Helpful Foods
- Foods high in omega-3 fatty acids for growth and repair of nervous tissue: nut, seed, cold water fish (salmon, halibut, mackerel) and vegetable oils (safflower, walnut, sunflower, flax seed), evening primrose oil (500 mg/3 times per day).
- Foods rich in vitamin B6—needed for normal brain function: Brewer's yeast, bok choy, spinach, banana, potato, whole grains.
- Foods rich in tryptophan—precursor to neurotransmitter serotonin: white turkey meat, milk, nuts, eggs, fish.
- Liver cleansing foods—proper liver function helps to regulate blood sugar: garlic, onions, broccoli, cauliflower, cabbage, Brussels sprouts, beets, carrots, artichokes, lemons, parsnips, dandelion greens, watercress, burdock root.
- Magnesium rich foods—important for nerve conduction: seeds, legumes, dark green leafy vegetables, soy products, almonds, pecans, cashews, wheat bran, meats.

Avoid
- Tobacco, alcohol, caffeine, artificial sweeteners
- Refined sugar and processed foods
- Be aware of your specific food sensitivities

Try a meal or snack with fiber-rich complex carbohydrates and low-fat protein to help balance your mood.

Spicy Tofu Salad
with Basalmic Dressing
makes four servings

1 pound firm-style tofu or Tempeh

3 cloves garlic, minced (separate into two small bowls)

Juice from 1 lemon

¼ tsp. chili flakes

½ tsp. chili powder

1 small jalapeno, seeded and minced

2 tbsp. olive oil

1 tbsp. basalmic vinegar

2 tsp. Dijon mustard

2 tsp. Maple syrup

4 cups organic salad greens including:

dandelion greens, watercress, arugula, baby kale, romaine, spinach, and swiss chard

½ cup organic shredded carrot

⅓ cup thinly sliced celery

¼ cup thinly sliced red onion

1 – 2 tablespoons canola oil

Binh Thanh Bui/Shutterstock.com

Drain tofu, cut into ½-inch thick slices, press briefly with paper towel to absorb excess water. If using tempeh, simply slice tempeh into ½-include slices.

In a shallow bowl, mix together half of the minced garlic, lemon juice, chili flakes, chili powder, and minced jalapeno; coat tofu/tempeh in liquid and allow it to marinate for 30 minutes. Drain and discard marinade; pat tofu/tempeh dry.

Preheat heavy iron skillet or wok. Lightly coat skillet with vegetable oil. Pan fry or stir fry tofu/tempeh for 4–5 minutes on each side or until lightly browned.

In small bowl, wisk together olive oil, basalmic vinegar, Dijon mustard, maple syrup, and the rest of the minced garlic.

Arrange salad greens on serving plates. Arrange tofu/tempeh evenly over greens. Garnish each salad with carrot, celery, and red onion. Top each portion with about 1 tablespoon of the dressing. Garnish, if you wish, with sliced jalapenos.

*Tofu and tempeh are good sources of magnesium. Deficiencies in magnesium have been linked to depression, irritability, and confusion.

REFERENCES

1. Alberts, B., Johnson, A., and Lewis, J. 2002. *How Cells Obtain Energy from Food*. [webpage] *National Institutes of Health*, 4th edition. [January 10, 2015]. Available from: http://www.ncbi.nlm.nih.gov/books/NBK26882/.

2. National Institute of Diabetes and Digestive and Kidney Diseases. 2013. *How Does Digestion Work?* [February 15, 2015]. Retrieved from: http://www.niddk.nih.gov/health-information/health-topics/Anatomy/your-digestive-system/Pages/anatomy.aspx.

3. Herman, C. P. and Polivy, J. 1984. "A Boundary Model for the Regulation of Eating." In *Eating and Its Disorders,* A. J. Stunkard & E. Stellar, eds. New York, NY: Raven Press, pp. 141–156.

4. Cisler, J. M., Olatunji, B., Feldner, M., and Forsyth, J. 2010. "Emotion Regulation and the Anxiety Disorders: An Integrative Review." *Journal of Psycholpathology and Behavioral Assessment* 32, pp. 68–82.

5. Uscher, J. 2005–2015. "3 Food Traps to Avoid When You're Depressed." [Webpage] *WebMD.* [February 5, 2015]. Available from: http://www.webmd.com/depression/features/depression-food-traps.

6. Gardner, M. P., Wansink, B., Kim, J., and Park, S.-B. 2014. "Better Moods for Better Eating?: How Mood Influences Food Choice." *Journal of Consumer Psychology* 24, pp. 320–335.

7. Margetic, S., Gazzola, C., Pegg, G. G., and Hill, R. A. 2002. "Leptin: A Review of Its Peripheral Actions and Interactions." *International Journal of Obesity* 26 (11), pp. 1407–1433.

8. Correia, M. L., and Haynes, W. G. 2004. "Leptin, Obesity and Cardiovascular Disease." *Current Opinion in Nephrology and Hypertension* 13, pp. 215–223.

9. Vasselli, J., Scarpace, P., Harris, R., and Banks, W. 2013. "Dietary Components in the Development of Leptin Resistance." *Advances in Nutrition* 4, pp. 164–175.

10. Shapiro, A., Tumer, N., Gao, Y., Cheng, K. Y., and Scarpace, P. J. 2011. "Prevention and Reversal of Diet-Induced Leptin Resistance with a Sugar-Free Diet Despite High-Fat Content." *Journal of Nutrition* 106 (3), pp. 390–397.

11. Lustig, R. 2012. *Fat Chance: Beating the Odds Against Sugar, Processed Food, Obesity, and Disease.* New York, NY: The Penguin Group.

12. National Diabetes Information Clearinghouse. 2014. "Insulin Resistance & Prediabetes." [Webpage] *Diabetes.niddk.nih.gov,* June. [February 17, 2015]. Available from: http://www.diabetes.niddk.nih.gov/dm/pubs/insulinresistance/index.aspx.

13. Koh, K., Park, S., and Quon, M. 2008. "Leptin and Cardiovascular Disease." *Contemporary Reviews in Cardiovascular Medicine* 117, pp. 3238–3249.

14. Prasad, C. 1998. "Food, Mood and Health: A Neurobiological Outlook." *Brazilian Journal of Medical and Biological Research* 31 (12), pp. 1517–1527.

15. Rogers, P. J. 1994. "Nutrition and Mental Performance." *Proceedings of the Nutrition Society* 53, pp. 443–456.

16. Spring, B. et al. 1983. "Effects of Protein and Carbohydrate Meals on Mood and Performance: Interactions with Sex and Age." *Journal of Psychiatric Research* 17 (2), p. 155.

17. Michaud, C., Musse, N., Nicolas, D., and Mejan, L. 1991. "Effects of Breakfast Size on Short-Term Memory Concentration and Blood Glucose." *Journal of Adolescent Health* 12, pp. 53–57.

18. Benton, D., and Donohoe, R. T. 1999. "The Effects of Nutrients on Mood." *Public Health Nutrition* 2, pp. 403–409.

19. Ottley, C. 2000. "Food and Mood." *Nursing Standard* 15, pp. 46–52.

20. Conklin, SM., Harris, JI., Manuck, SB., and Yao, JK. 2007. "Serum omega-3 Fatty Acids Are Associated With Variation In Mood, Personality, and Behavior in Hypercholesterolemic Community Volunteers." *Psychiatry Res.,* 152(1), pp. 1–10.

MINDFUL EATING REFLECTION JOURNAL

1. Acknowledge
Describe your experience; what did you choose to eat?

2. Intentional Attention

Describe what you noticed during your mindful eating practice.

BREATH:	
BODY:	
EMOTIONS:	
THOUGHTS:	
SENSES:	

3. Accept Without Judgment
Describe judgment; acceptance

4. Choose Your Experience
Intention/willingness; new perspective

5. Mindful Meditation/Mindful Eating Experience (Mindful Practice)
What did you notice about your meditation experience this week?

MINDFUL EATING WEEKLY QUIZ

This is a brief snapshot of your mindful eating skills. It is to help you to identify which skills you may want to change or enhance. Circle the best answer. Don't forget to notice what you already do well. After you complete this quiz, write down a mindful eating goal for the week.

Take this quiz each week of the course.

---

1. I tend to stop eating when I am full

All of the time   Most of the time   Occasionally   Sometimes   Almost Never

---

2. I eat when I am hungry rather than when I feel emotional

All of the time   Most of the time   Occasionally   Sometimes   Almost Never

---

3. I try not to "pick" at food

All of the time   Most of the time   Occasionally   Sometimes   Almost Never

---

4. I taste each bite before reaching for the next

All of the time   Most of the time   Occasionally   Sometimes   Almost Never

---

5. When I eat, I think about how nourishing the food is for my body

All of the time   Most of the time   Occasionally   Sometimes   Almost Never

---

6. I am nonjudgmental of myself, my body and when I accidentally overeat

All of the time   Most of the time   Occasionally   Sometimes   Almost Never

---

7. I don't multitask while I eat. When I eat, I just eat and focus on the food in front of me

All of the time   Most of the time   Occasionally   Sometimes   Almost Never

---

8. I don't have to eat everything on my plate, I can leave what I don't want

All of the time   Most of the time   Occasionally   Sometimes   Almost Never

---

9. I tend to eat slowly, chewing each bite

All of the time   Most of the time   Occasionally   Sometimes   Almost Never

---

10. I recognize when I slip into mindless eating (zoned out, popping food into my mouth)

All of the time   Most of the time   Occasionally   Sometimes   Almost Never

---

List your Mindful Eating Goals: (ex: learn to be more present when I eat, slow down, stop when I'm full)

The Truth About Sugar

Courtesy of Maria Napoli

> *Sugary Sweets, tempting and alluring*
> *I see it*
> *I smell it*
> *I want it*
> *I eat it*
> *What next?*
> *I see it*
> *I smell it*
> *I want it*
> *I think about it*
> *Sometimes I say yes and often I say no*
>
> (Napoli)

"I tried every kind of dieting. They said decrease your calories; increase your exercise; you're lazy; you're stressed out. And then I met Dr. Lustig. He said it was none of those things. It was all the sugar and it was a lack of fiber. I changed my food to the things that he told me to do. I've lost 100 pounds; I've restored my vitality, my health, and I'm happy" (1.)

Sugar is an amazing substance. It is pure sensation, pleasure in a crystalline form. We share as humans a desire for its innate sweetness, which begins at mother's breast. This taste of milk sugar is the fuel that energizes all of life—white gold—pure carbohydrate energy that moves our bodies. The calories in a cup of breast milk are nearly 40% from sugar in the form of lactose (2). The deep and primal appeal of sugar is one of the reasons that sugar and sugar-filled foods are now among the most popular and commonly chosen edibles. In the past, sugar was expensive and rare, and consumption was limited to the wealthy and was reserved for the end of a meal. Now sugar is cheap and abundant, with manufactured sugars infused in nearly every packaged product sold in supermarkets. Like most good things in life, it is best in moderation, and easy to over consume without realizing it, especially in a manufactured, processed form.

What We Know About Sugar

Sugar has been around for thousands of years. Its earliest form of consumption other than mother's milk is most likely fruit(3). Dates are nearly 60% sugar, and other types of fruits become very sweet when dried out. The most concentrated source of natural sweetness is honey, which is the stored food of bees, and it is 80% sugar (3). Honey collection has been represented in ancient cave paintings that are 10,000 years old, and domesticizing bees for honey production may be a 4,000-year-old practice. The drive for sugar is biologically based, with mother's milk affording exceptional immunity from its consumption, as well as being the stuff of life. No wonder we can't get enough of it!

We look to history to learn how humans for centuries have become slaves to sugar. Has this enslavement to sweetness turned into subjugation? Books have been written about sugar's presence throughout history, where people found ways around geography, technological difficulties, and even political strife in order to feed their need for sugar. In the early history of the Americas Christopher Columbus brought sugar cane along to the New World where it became cultivated in Spanish Santo Domingo, converted into granulated sugar by African slaves, and then shipped back to Europe beginning in 1516 to meet the insatiable demand (3). In 1807, a British naval blockade of France cut off access to sugar cane crops, and businessmen learned quickly how to extract sugar from beets, in order to meet the demand.

Michael Rosskothen/Shutterstock.com

REMEMBER—UNDERSTAND—DECIDE

Until 1970, cane and beets were the two main sources of sugar, but rising prices moved business to invent a cheaper way to produce sweetness, and high-fructose corn syrup was born. Refined sugar (i.e., sucrose) is made up of a molecule of the carbohydrate glucose, bonded to a molecule of the carbohydrate fructose—a 50–50 mixture of the two. The fructose, which is almost twice as sweet as glucose, is what distinguishes sugar from other carbohydrate-rich foods such as bread or potatoes that break down upon digestion to glucose alone (4). The more fructose in a substance, the sweeter it will be.

panda3800/Shutterstock.com

The Turtle Factory/Shutterstock.com

High-fructose corn syrup, as it is most commonly consumed, is 55% fructose, and the remaining 45% is nearly all glucose (5). It was first marketed in the late 1970s and was created to be indistinguishable from refined sugar when used in soft drinks. Because each of these sugars ends up as glucose and fructose in our system, our bodies respond the same way to both, and the physiological effects are identical.

WHAT HAPPENS WHEN FRUCTOSE AND GLUCOSE MOVE THROUGH OUR BODY?

Human Liver Anatomy

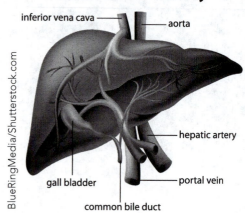

inferior vena cava —

— aorta

— hepatic artery

gall bladder —

— portal vein

common bile duct

BlueRingMedia/Shutterstock.com

This mix of fructose and glucose wreaks havoc on the body's metabolism: glucose is metabolized by cells all through the body (just like the sugars in breast milk); fructose is processed primarily in the liver. Take a breath. Mindfully bring an image of your liver into focus, a key organ to optimal health. Mindfully pay attention to and understand this process. Our liver has a big job to do. It not only is working to break down the sugars, it also shares the job of breaking down fat with the gall bladder as well as eliminating many substances we put in our body that we do not need. If you eat too much sugar in quickly digested forms such as candy and soda, the liver breaks down the fructose and produces fats called triglycerides. Some triglycerides are stored in the liver, but many are pushed out into the bloodstream. This elevates blood pressure, and leads to something called insulin resistance, when our cells become non-responsive to insulin, so the pancreas pumps more and more insulin into the blood trying to keep things in balance. Metabolic syndrome develops, signaled by abdominal obesity ("belly fat"); high-blood pressure, and other changes that may lead to Type 2 Diabetes increasing the risk of heart attack and stroke. Mindfully decide what your body needs.

In animals, or at least in laboratory rats and mice, it's clear that if the fructose hits the liver in sufficient quantity and with sufficient speed, the liver will convert much of it to fat. This apparently induces a condition known as insulin resistance, which is now considered the fundamental problem in obesity, and the underlying defect in heart disease and in the type of diabetes, type 2 that is common to obese and overweight individuals. It might also be the underlying defect in many cancers.

If what happens in laboratory rodents also happens in humans, and if we are eating enough sugar to make it happen, then we are in trouble (6).

OVERDOSING ON HIGH-FRUCTOSE CORN SYRUP: ARE YOU A VICTIM?

Initially embraced by the soda industry, with its cost artificially low due to governmental price subsidies for corn, this liquid sweetener became pumped into nearly every manufactured packaged product. During this same period (1970–2000), our consumption of sugar-sweetened soda doubled to 40 gallons a

The Turtle Factory/Shutterstock.com

year per person at its peak in 2010 (3). Did you know that one can of soda has about 10 teaspoons of sugar! Always diversifying, soda manufacturers found ways to keep up with the creation of new versions of sweet drinks, including teas, exercise drinks, vitamin water, and energy drinks. We now consume nearly 14 gallons a person per year of these "enhanced" beverages. It is ordinary table sugar (sucrose), and our ability to manufacture cheap forms of it has led to problems of excess which some experts believe are responsible for most of today's health problems.

An Alarming Epidemic

America is addicted to sugar, with over 100 pounds consumed yearly by every man, woman, and child. It's throughout our food supply (77% of the foods in the American food supply include added sugar), and plays a huge role in metabolic syndrome, which leads to diseases such as diabetes. One research study showed that while eating an extra 150 calories per day did not increase diabetes prevalence worldwide, if those calories came from soda, diabetes prevalence went up 11-fold for the same number of calories (7).

The Department of Health and Human Services states that increased consumption of added sugars, which are sweeteners added to food and beverages, has been linked to obesity and a decrease in the intake of essential vitamins and minerals. One study revealed that an average U.S. adult consumes 21.4 teaspoons of *added sugar* each and every day, representing 16% of total daily calorie intake (7). This added sugar does not take into account additional sugar in fruit juices, fruits, or other whole foods. Among children, the numbers are similar, with about 16% of daily calories consumed in the form of added sugar. Some surveys suggest teenagers may be eating far more—up to 34 teaspoons a day.

The United States Department of Agriculture (USDA) recommends for women consume no more than 6 teaspoons of added sugars per day, and men no more than 9 teaspoons. Since many foods include a combination of added sugars and naturally occurring sugars from fruit and dairy, we have no easy way to identify the amount of sugars added to products we buy at the supermarket. Nutrition labels do not indicate how much sugar has been added, and food manufacturers don't voluntarily disclose this information.

How much sugar is too much? The American Heart Association (AHA) recommends that added sugar intake make up no more than half of your daily *discretionary* calories (not *total* calories), which means about 6 teaspoons of sugar for women and 9 teaspoons for men (8). Other experts, like Dr. Robert Lustig, argue that this is too much.

Calories from Added Sugars in Commonly Purchased Foods	
Food	Calories from Added Sugars per Serving
Carbonated soda (12 oz. can)	132.5
Canned peaches in heavy syrup (1 cup)	115.4
Jelly beans (10 large)	78.4
Non-fat fruit yogurt (6 oz. container)	77.5
Milk chocolate, 1 bar (1.55 oz)	77.4

Calories from Added Sugars in Commonly Purchased Foods	
Food	Calories from Added Sugars per Serving
Cake doughnut (1)	74.2
Sweetened condensed milk (1 fl oz)	73.8
Fruit punch drink (12 oz can)	62.1
Angel food cake (1 piece)	60.4
Chocolate puff cereal (1 cup)	56.4
Vanilla ice cream (1/2 cup)	48.0
Pancake syrup (1 tbsp)	26.5
Chocolate chip cookies (1)	13.6
Cinnamon raisin bagel (4″ diameter)	12.8

Dr. Robert Lustig is a pediatric endocrinologist from University of California, San Francisco. He believes that sugar is toxic and should be regulated like tobacco and alcohol in order to protect public health. In a report published in the journal *Nature*, he contends that sugar is contributing to 35 million deaths worldwide each year due to obesity and diseases such as diabetes, heart disease, and cancer (7).

Dr. Lustig believes it is more than just the empty calories of sugar that are dangerous. He believes that sugar is toxic to the body, and calories are not the issue. Health risks from excess sugar include changes in metabolism, increased blood pressure, liver damage, and interference with hormone signaling. Lustig argues that eating too much sugar, in fact, also causes many of the health effects caused by drinking too much alcohol (6).

For example, too much sugar is associated with high cholesterol, which is known to increase heart disease risk. One study found that those who got 25% or more of their daily calories from sugar had double the risk of having low HDL (good) cholesterol compared to those who consumed less than 5% of their calories as sugar (3). Those who ate the most sugar also had the highest triglyceride levels (low HDL and high triglycerides are two of the primary risk factors for heart disease).

Sugar is also linked to cancer (9–14). High blood sugar levels, caused by health conditions such as diabetes along with eating too many sugary foods, have been linked to cancers of the pancreas, skin, uterus, urinary tract, and breast. Women with the highest blood sugar levels were found to have a 26% higher risk of developing cancer than those with the lowest (15), whereas women with the highest carbohydrate intake (62% of their diet or more) were more than twice as likely to develop breast cancer than those with a lower carb intake (52% or less) (16).

Nutrition Labeling: Why It Matters

Your body doesn't need to get any carbohydrate from added sugar. That's why the Healthy Eating Pyramid says sugary drinks and sweets should be used sparingly, if at all, and the Healthy Eating Plate does not include foods with added sugars.

Rangizzz/Shutterstock.com

4 grams of sugar = 1 teaspoon—an important fact to keep in mind when reading nutrition labels

The average American consumes 22 teaspoons of added sugar a day, which amounts to an extra 350 calories (17). While we sometimes add sugar to food ourselves, most added sugar comes from processed and prepared foods. Sugar-sweetened beverages and breakfast cereals are two of the most serious offenders.

The AHA has recommended that Americans drastically cut back on added sugar to help slow the obesity and heart disease epidemics (8).

- The AHA suggests an added-sugar limit of no more than 100 calories per day (about 6 teaspoons or 24 grams of sugar) for most women and no more than 150 calories per day (about 9 teaspoons or 36 grams of sugar) for most men.
- There's no nutritional need or benefit that comes from eating added sugar. A good rule of thumb is to avoid products that have a lot of added sugar, including skipping foods that list "sugar" as the first or second ingredient. However, the growing use of alternative sweeteners can make it difficult to determine which ingredients count as sugar, because there are multiple sources of sugar with different names.

Type of Sugar: Does It Matter?

The bottom line is sugar is sugar no matter what form it comes in. Our bodies identify sugar whether it is processed, fruit, raw, organic, or otherwise. White versus brown? Raw versus refined? Organic or not? When it comes to sugar, there are a lot of options but choosing raw or organic sugar will not change the health risks (with the exception of perhaps lowering pesticide and chemical exposure for organic brands). There are some slight differences——for instance, unrefined raw sugar is made from the juice of the sugar cane plant, and as it is not fully refined, it will have trace minerals and nutrients, although not in any significant amounts——but they are negligible in terms of your health.

Derek Hatfield/Shutterstock.com

FIGURE 1. By law, The Nutrition Facts Label must list the grams of sugar in each product. But some foods naturally contain sugar, while others get theirs from added sweeteners, and food labeling laws don't require companies to differentiate how much sugar is added sugar.

How do you know the amount of what is in the food you are eating? When reading the nutrition facts label, ingredients are listed in order of predominance by weight. This means that the product contains more of the first ingredient than any other *single* ingredient. So if the ingredients are "oats, honey, peanut butter, water, salt", you know that there are more oats than honey in the product, even if only by a tiny margin. However, it's possible that if you combine the honey and peanut butter, they outweigh the oats.

Remember that sugar can be listed under various names (since, strictly speaking, they're different foods), so manufacturers will frequently use more than one type of sugar so they can move them further down the list. For example, if the manufacturer decides to use honey and maple syrup as the sweeteners instead of just honey, the ingredients list might look more like this: "oats, peanut butter, honey, maple syrup, water, salt." It can be the same amount of sugar as the first example, but now they've gotten peanut butter moved up on the list (and sugar moved down).

Sugar: MAC Your Experience . . .

It can be overwhelming to think about all of the types of sugar that exists in our food. You might consider yourself to be a healthy eater, and now you're confused. You've tried hard, you've made mistakes, and now you're sitting with blame and judgment as you read this section. Right now, in this moment, breathe into your experience and have a mindful MAC moment (18) as you

1. Acknowledge the feelings you have about this new information regarding sugar
2. pay attention to the feelings that arise
3. accept your feelings (whether they be disappointment, confusion, anger, sadness) without judgment, and
4. make a choice to take skillful action.

Remember, once you notice, then you have an opportunity to change.

It can be really hard to spot those added sugars. Below is a list of the most common types of sugars. Do not let some of their healthy-sounding names fool you: *refined sugar is refined sugar!*

This is not a complete list, but it covers the vast majority of names for sugar.

1. Fruit juice concentrate
2. Fruit juice

3. Sugar
4. Invert sugar
5. Cane sugar
6. Cane juice
7. Evaporated cane juice
8. Raw cane sugar
9. Brown sugar
10. Beet sugar
11. Palm sugar
12. Date sugar
13. Coconut sugar
14. Barley malt (Manufacturers love this one because it doesn't have the words "syrup" or "sugar" in the name)
15. Malt syrup
16. Rice bran syrup
17. Corn syrup
18. Corn syrup solids
19. High fructose corn syrup
20. Dextrose
21. Maltodextrin
22. Glucose
23. Glucose solids
24. Fructose
25. Sucrose
26. Maltose
27. Lactose
28. Galactose
29. Honey
30. Maple syrup
31. Agave
32. Sorghum syrup
33. Diastatic malt
34. Molasses
35. Caramel
36. Treacle
37. Golden syrup
38. Panocha
39. Muscovado sugar
40. Turbinado sugar
41. Demerara sugar
42. Sucanat
43. Rapadura
44. Jaggery
45. Panela
46. Monk fruit/Luo Han Guo

Added Sugars: Why It Matters?

"71% of the added sugars in Americans' diets come from grocery bought foods," said Dr. Adam Drewnowski, Director of the Nutritional Sciences Program at the University of Washington. According to Dr. Drewnowski, it is essential to find tools to implement that help us move toward healthier diets (19).

One such tool you might want to explore to help you become better educated in assessing how much sugar is in the food you are eating is called Tracking Added Sugars by Fooducate (www.fooducate .com). Analyzing over 250,000 grocery products in Fooducate's database developed this tracking tool. A series of sophisticated algorithms were used to evaluate nutrients and ingredients in products, resulting in an accurate estimate of added sugar content.

It can be surprising to learn how much sugar has been added to processed food. With awareness comes choice——once we know, we have the opportunity to change and move to a more healthful diet. By pinpointing the foods that contain excessive amounts of added sugars and swapping them with healthier choices, we can help ourselves through technology tools to take a simple and significant step toward improving our diets.

5 Healthy Sugar Substitutes That Won't Sabotage Your Health

The next time you're wanting a sweet treat, one of the healthiest options may be to make your own at home, using the healthier options below. You'll notice that artificial sweeteners are not on this list, as many have some concerning health issues in their own right. These natural substances can add a little healthy sweetness to your everyday meals and baked treats without sacrificing your health:

- **Stevia:** A sweet Central and South American herb
- **Raw honey(sparingly):** Although still a high source of sugar, raw honey contains antioxidants, minerals, enzymes, vitamins, and phytonutrients
- **Applesauce:** Look for an unsweetened brand, as apples are naturally sweet (or make your own)
- **Raisins or dates:** Chop them up finely to add sweetness to cereal, cookies, and other baked goods
- **Pureed ripe bananas:** A natural way to add sweetness to baked goods

Dr. Lustig has some recommendations, too. His Do's and Don'ts apply to nutritional intake overall, and avoids excess sugars.

Do
- Shop the edges of the store, not aisles for real food
- Eat more omega-3 fatty acids, found in wild fish and flax
- Eat fruit as dessert, and if you're craving cookies or cake, make your own
- Increase consumption of micronutrients, the vitamins and minerals found in fruits and vegetables
- Up your fiber intake. Fiber protects your liver from sugar, says Lustig, and keeps you from overeating
- Eat more whole grains such as farro, quinoa, steel-cut oats, hulled barley, or brown rice

Don't
- Drink your calories. Avoid soda, sports drinks, and juice
- Shop hungry—it leads to poor food choices
- Eat anything with "partially hydrogenated" in the ingredient list. That means it contains trans-fat, which our bodies can't metabolize and ends up lining our arteries
- Buy anything that has sugar as one of the first three ingredients
- Eat corn-fed beef or farmed fish. Corn oil contains omega-6 fatty acids, which lead to inflammation
- Buy processed food. "If it comes with a label," says Lustig, "think of it as a warning label" (1).

Enjoy this healthy treat the next time you're in the mood for a sweet food. Filled with antioxidants, micronutrients, calcium, and fiber, it will neutralize your craving and provide valuable nutrition.

Cantaloupe Smoothie

This easy and delicious dessert in a glass is sweetened with dates. Dates provide 50% more potassium than bananas and are a wonderful source of fiber. Molasses, an old-fashioned sweetener, provides many essential micronutrients including calcium and iron.

Serves 1

1½ cups unsweetened plant-based milk

1 teaspoon unsulfured molasses

6 Medjool dates, pitted and chopped

2 cups chopped cantaloupe

2 to 3 ice cubes

Combine all ingredients in a blender and process until smooth and creamy.

Garnish with fresh mint.

References

1. Lustig, R. H., Millar, H., and Gershen, C. 2014. *The Fat Chance Cookbook: More than 100 Recipes Ready in Under 30 Minutes to Help You Lose the Sugar and the Weight.* New York, NY: Hudson Street Press.
2. McGee, H. 2004. *On Food and Cooking: The Science and Lore of the Kitchen.* Completely Rev. & Updated ed. New York, NY: Scribner.
3. Cohen, R. 2013. "Sugar." [Webpage] *National Geographic.* [January 4, 2015]. Available from: http://ngm.nationalgeographic.com/2013/08/sugar/cohen-text.
4. Poplawski, S., and Pezzuto, M. 1997. "Isomerization of Glucose to Fructose." [Webpage]. [February 18, 2015]. Available from: http://www.rpi.edu/dept/chem-eng/Biotech-Environ/IMMOB/poppezz/hfcs.html.
5. US Food and Drug Administration. 2014. "High Fructose Corn Syrup: Questions and Answers." *Food Additives and Ingredients.* [Webpage]. [February 18, 2015]. Available from: http://www.fda.gov/Food/IngredientsPackagingLabeling/FoodAdditivesIngredients/ucm324856.htm.
6. Taubes, G. 2011. "Is Sugar Toxic?" [Website] *The New York Times Magazine*, April 13. [December 5, 2014]. Available from: http://www.nytimes.com/2011/04/17/magazine/mag-17Sugar-t.html?pagewanted=all&_r=0.
7. Pope, S. 2014. "Sweet Revenge: Dr Robert Lustig Explains How to Cut Sugar, Lose Weight, and Turn the Tables on Processed Foods." [Webpage] *KQED*, August 6. [February 3, 2015]. Available from: http://blogs.kqed.org/bayareabites/2014/08/06/sweet-revenge-dr-robert-lustig-explains-how-to-cut-sugar-lose-weight-and-turn-the-tables-on-processed-foods/.
8. American Heart Association. 2014. "Sugar 101." [Website]. [December 30, 2014]. Available from: http://www.heart.org/HEARTORG/GettingHealthy/NutritionCenter/HealthyEating/Sugar-101_UCM_306024_Article.jsp.
9. Warburg, O. 1956. "On the Origin of Cancer Cells." *Science* 123, pp. 309–314.
10. Volk, T. et al. 1993. "pH in Human Tumor Xenografts: Effect of Intravenous Administration of Glucose." *British Journal of Cancer* 68 (3), pp. 492–500.
11. Digirolamo, M. 1994. *Diet and Cancer: Markers, Prevention and Treatment.* New York, NY: Plenum Press. p. 203.
12. Leeper, D. B. et al. 1998. "Effect of i.v. Glucose Versus Combined i.v. plus Oral Glucose on Human Tumor Extracellular pH for Potential Sensitization to Thermoradiotherapy." *International Journal of Hyperthermia* 14 (3), pp. 257–269.
13. Rossi-Fanelli, F. et al. 1991. "Abnormal Substrate Metabolism and Nutritional Strategies in Cancer Management." *Journal of Parenteral and Enteral Nutrition* 15 (6), pp. 680–683.

14. Grant, J. P. 1990. "Proper Use and Recognized Role of TPN in the Cancer Patient." *Nutrition* 6 (4 Suppl), pp. 6S–7S, 10S.

15. Larsson, S., Bergkvist, L., and Wolk, A. 2006. "Consumption of Sugar and Sugar-Sweetened Foods and the Risk of Pancreatic Cancer in a Prospective Study." *The American Journal of Clinical Nutrition* 84 (5), pp. 1171–1176.

16. Lajous, M., Boutron-Rualt, M., Fabre, A., Clavel-Chapelon, F., and Romieu, I. 2008. "Carbohydrate Intake, Glycemic Index, Glycemic Load, and Risk of Postmenopausal Breast Cancer in a Prospective Study of French Women." *American Journal of Clinical Nutrition* 87, pp. 1384–1391.

17. Harvard School of Public Health. 2015. "Added Sugar in the Diet." [Webpage] *The Nutrition Source.* [January 10, 2015]. Available from: http://www.hsph.harvard.edu/nutritionsource/carbohydrates/added-sugar-in-the-diet/#ref27.

18. Napoli, M. 2011. *Tools for Mindful Living: Steppingstones for Practice.* Dubuque, IA: Kendall Hunt Publishing.

19. Drewnowski, A., and Darmon, N. 2005. "The Economics of Obesity: Dietary Energy Density and Energy Cost." *American Journal of Clinical Nutrition* 82, pp. 2655–273S.

MINDFUL EATING REFLECTION JOURNAL

1. Acknowledge
Describe your experience; what did you choose to eat?

2. Intentional Attention

Describe what you noticed during your mindful eating practice.

BREATH:
BODY:
EMOTIONS:
THOUGHTS:
SENSES:

3. Accept Without Judgment
Describe judgment; acceptance

4. Choose Your Experience
Intention/willingness; new perspective

5. Mindful Meditation/Mindful Eating Experience (Mindful Practice)
What did you notice about your meditation experience this week?

MINDFUL EATING WEEKLY QUIZ

This is a brief snapshot of your mindful eating skills. It is to help you to identify which skills you may want to change or enhance. Circle the best answer. Don't forget to notice what you already do well. After you complete this quiz, write down a mindful eating goal for the week.

Take this quiz each week of the course.

1. I tend to stop eating when I am full				
←				→
All of the time	Most of the time	Occasionally	Sometimes	Almost Never
2. I eat when I am hungry rather than when I feel emotional				
All of the time	Most of the time	Occasionally	Sometimes	Almost Never
3. I try not to "pick" at food				
All of the time	Most of the time	Occasionally	Sometimes	Almost Never
4. I taste each bite before reaching for the next				
All of the time	Most of the time	Occasionally	Sometimes	Almost Never
5. When I eat, I think about how nourishing the food is for my body				
All of the time	Most of the time	Occasionally	Sometimes	Almost Never
6. I am nonjudgmental of myself, my body and when I accidentally overeat				
All of the time	Most of the time	Occasionally	Sometimes	Almost Never
7. I don't multitask while I eat. When I eat, I just eat and focus on the food in front of me				
All of the time	Most of the time	Occasionally	Sometimes	Almost Never
8. I don't have to eat everything on my plate, I can leave what I don't want				
All of the time	Most of the time	Occasionally	Sometimes	Almost Never
9. I tend to eat slowly, chewing each bite				
All of the time	Most of the time	Occasionally	Sometimes	Almost Never
10. I recognize when I slip into mindless eating (zoned out, popping food into my mouth)				
All of the time	Most of the time	Occasionally	Sometimes	Almost Never
List your Mindful Eating Goals: (ex: learn to be more present when I eat, slow down, stop when I'm full)				

CHAPTER 5

The Truth About Fat, Sugar, and Salt: The War for Your Taste buds

Courtesy of Maria Napoli

Sometimes it is a battle
Everything looks delicious
I'm drawn to taste it all
I take a mindful moment
My mindless monster is silenced
I make a conscious choice

(Napoli)

"I think we've made nutrition increasingly confusing. It's very hard to see what is real food. And I think we need to move back to a simpler time, where we're focused on eating real foods—fruits and vegetables and whole grains. It sounds so simple, but it's hard to do, because our behavior has become so conditioned and driven by fat, sugar, and salt that's loaded and layered into our foods, and our brains are constantly being bombarded with food cues."
—*Dr. David Kessler, The End of Overeating*

There is a war underway for your food preferences and eating habits. Much like modern combat, which is waged in stealth mode, the battle for your taste buds is insidious and covert. Food scientists and marketers spend nearly all of their waking hours finding ways to hijack your taste buds and drive you to consume highly processed, unhealthy food (1). Deliberately manipulating the formula of manufactured food products to cultivate taste preferences, this war is a battle for your spending dollars. Some argue it is a battle for your health, and even your life (2).

Do you wonder why it is so hard to resist the allure of processed foods? Defined as foods that are packaged in boxes, cans, or bags, these foods need to be worked using machines and chemicals to be edible and are not found as in nature. In addition to going through many complex steps, processed foods often contain additives, artificial flavorings, and other chemical ingredients (3). They are impossible to resist. Exerting a powerful siren call, and designed to include just the right combination of fat, sugar, and salt, processed foods make us crave and seek more and more. We eat unconsciously; beyond the point of satiety, beyond fullness. We are engaged in a battle for our hearts and minds, since a diet of mostly processed, manufactured food is associated with poor health outcomes including obesity, Type 2 diabetes, cardiac heart disease, hypertension, and early death (4). The ability to resist the siren call of fake foods is literally a fight for our lives.

Fat, Sugar, and Salt in the "Right" Combination

About two-thirds of adults in the United States are overweight (5). The number of overweight and obese children is also growing at an alarming rate. These trends have adverse consequences on health because obesity increases the risk of chronic diseases, notably diabetes, cardiovascular diseases, obstructive sleep apnea, and cancer (6). Obesity is also a major cause of disability and mental health issues (7) (including anxiety and depression) and may shorten lifespan (8).

Unraveling the factors underlying the rising incidence of obesity is complex, as we've seen in earlier chapters. The former chairman of the Food and Drug Administration (FDA), Dr. David Kessler, has developed a theory worth considering: Modern foods, particularly American foods, are designed not to satisfy, but rather to stimulate the reward pathways in the brain, conditioning us to crave more food in a behavioral pattern he calls conditioned hypereating (9).

If we identify sugar, fat, and salt as the major culprits of modern (American) food responsible for heightening our appetites, inducing overeating, and causing excessive weight gain, we can explain why we have difficulty maintaining normal weight in a land of plentiful processed food. Kessler reminds us how sugar, fat, and salt activate neurons involved in taste perception, reward, and conscious control of eating. The key brain hormones involved are dopamine and opioids, which mediate the rewiring of brain circuits (10). It becomes easy to explain how eating in modern society no longer serves a primary function of satisfying hunger and replenishing energy stores. Rather, eating serves a hedonic (pleasure driven) role to satisfy our liking and wanting of food. Most of us eat out of habit instead of physiological need. This behavior is controlled by social, cultural, and other environmental cues.

SPECIAL FOODS TO FEED OUR BRAINS— LEADING TO OVEREATING

To hijack our reward systems, the food industry has developed hyper stimulating foods, packaging and marketing them in ways that appeal to our altered brain chemistry (11). Processed foods are laden with sugar, fat, and salt; the list of ingredients is often misleading; and food texture has been altered to make it easier to eat faster. Examples of this in practice include potato chips, chopped-up meats, and cookies that are designed to manipulate the brain response and entice us to eat more. Following exposure to these hyper stimulating foods, some individuals simply cannot control their eating behavior.

PHYSICAL CRAVING AND FOOD ADDICTION

Craving and addiction researchers are turning their scientific attention to the study of food preferences and the desire to eat more and more. Beyond looking at ways we are deliberately manipulated into buying more food products through advertising and taste preferences, psychologists investigating binge eating disorder in the 1990s first suspected that the physical craving binge eaters report is a direct result of eating certain types of food (12). Researchers explained how physical craving describes an experience different from normal hunger. The addiction model of physical craving for certain foods suggests that a person eats a food, and then wants to eat more even though they had not expected to want more before they started eating. Or, the person eats food, and after a period of not eating it, has a stronger desire for the food even though by all objective standards they are "full".

Many researchers have looked at specific components of processed food, especially salt, sugar, and fat to see if the addiction model can explain why we habitually overeat these ingredients. One study (13) gave rats a 25% sugar solution with rat chow for 12 hours, and then took away their chow for the next 12 hours. Repeating this pattern of excessive sugar intake, then deprivation, for a period of 30 days, their brains were

measured to see if their pleasure receptors in the brain showed any changes. Just like drug addiction, the rat brains showed desensitization in the pleasure centers following periods of excessive sugar intake, indicating a pattern seen with certain drugs of abuse. We know from this type of research that daily bingeing on sugar releases dopamine in the pleasure centers of our brains, and this binge pattern can drive us to consume more and more to get the same "pleasure" because we become desensitized to the "addictive" substance (in this case sugar, in other cases, drugs such as cocaine or opiates).

Hooked on Salt?

There is an American love affair with salt. According to many experts, including the American Heart Association (14), we eat too much of it. So much so that the FDA is thinking about limiting the amount of sodium in packaged foods.

Cutting back on sodium would almost certainly be good for the country's health. The average American consumes nearly 50 % more sodium than experts recommend, most of it from processed foods (15).

Though it adds flavor and helps preserve food, excess sodium can cause high blood pressure and increase the risk of heart attack, stroke, and other health problems. Even though sodium is found in nature, too much sodium added to our foods results in serious health consequences. Some of the problems include stiffening our arteries, so the heart has to pump harder and harder to circulate blood. The kidneys, whose job is to clean the body of excess compounds, including salt, have to work harder and harder and wear out. Even though the body has a beautiful design as a self-regulating machine engineered to perfectly balance our own levels of salt, it was never designed to handle the enormous amounts we eat, primarily because of processed and fast food.

WHY NOT JUST CUT BACK ON SALT?

Experts tell us that the American palate has become so accustomed to the high levels of sodium and salt added to our meals that the only way to kick the habit might be to wean ourselves off it slowly. If we stop using salt and go cold turkey, there is a significant change in the taste of the food. For most of us, taste is the most important reason why we eat something. If we lower sodium abruptly, food wouldn't taste good.

How We Got Hooked on Sodium

Along with sweet, sour, bitter, and umami (a Japanese word that roughly translates as "savory"), salt is one of the five basic tastes recognized by human taste buds. Just as some people have a sweet tooth and some don't, some people crave that salty taste more than others.

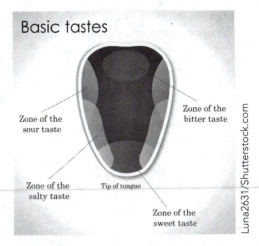

Basic tastes

Zone of the sour taste

Zone of the bitter taste

Zone of the salty taste

Tip of tongue

Zone of the sweet taste

Experts are still trying to untangle the factors that influence an individual's appetite for saltiness.

Some appear to be biological. Studies suggest that babies whose mothers suffer from morning sickness tend to have above-average salt appetites, because vomiting depletes sodium levels in the body (16). Other studies have explored whether individual preferences may be related to stress, anxiety, or even personality traits (17). Habit likely plays a much bigger role in salt preference (18). As with any of our eating habits, if we get accustomed to saltier food, we need to maintain that level to continue to enjoy our meals and feel satisfied.

The increasing levels of sodium in our diets—and especially in processed foods—over the past several decades have created what amounts to a "cultural addiction" to the taste of salt (19). However, just as we tend to get used to increased amounts of salt and sodium, we are also are relatively quick to adjust to the taste of a diet lower in salt.

Studies show that people who switch to reduced-sodium diets develop a heightened sensitivity to saltiness within about 2 to 3 months, and therefore need less salt to get the same pleasure from their food (19).

More than three-quarters of our sodium intake comes from processed foods, while only about 6% comes from the saltshakers on our dinner tables (20). Even if you don't add salt to your food, your intake of sodium is likely much higher than healthy if you eat processed or fast food.

Balancing Sodium and Potassium: Intake of salt and potassium must be in balance for both minerals to provide maximum health benefits

Health Benefits of Salt and Potassium

Salt provides two elements——sodium and chloride—both of which are essential for life. Your body cannot make these elements on its own, so you *must* get them from your diet.

The debate about the dangers of eating too much salt has gained a new wrinkle: A federal study suggests that the people most at risk are those who also get too little potassium (21). Potassium-rich foods, including fruits and vegetables, are recommended as a dietary defense against heart disease and other chronic illnesses. A research study looking at the relationship of salt, potassium, and heart disease deaths shows that if you have too much sodium and too little potassium, it's worse than either on its own (22).

This is because potassium may neutralize the negative effects of salt, including the heart-damaging effects of too much salt in the diet. We know that sodium increases the risk of high blood pressure, a major cause of heart disease and stroke.

Study findings show that people who eat a lot of salt and very little potassium are more than twice as likely to die from a heart attack as those who ate about equal amounts of both (23). This imbalance of nutrients poses a greater risk than simply eating too much salt.

Isn't All This Just Confusing Crazy Talk?

Here's what matters: there is a tremendous amount of confusion about salt—how much is too much, whether or not going "cold turkey" with excess salt is satisfying, and how to take skillful action. One thing is certain: many of these confusing messages are coming from those who are hurt the most if we cut back on salt: the *food industry* (24). Their messaging machine is in high gear, making sure our confusion turns into passive inaction. Not held accountable for their actions, they endanger the lives of children and adults, hooking our taste buds and creating salt addicts for life, shortening our life spans. What's a mindful person to do?

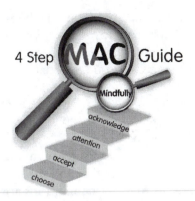

Mindfulness Matters: How It Helps

Know what matters. *Excess salt is harming the health of Americans.* The research is unequivocal and undeniable (25). *Most sources of salt in our diets come from processed foods and fast foods.* The research is clear: processed foods are designed to alter our taste buds, and habituate us to eat more and more in ways that change our brain chemistry (26).

Take skillful action. It is important to remember that there are vested interests in the battle for our taste buds—lobbyists and insiders for the food industry love to confuse us, keep us coming back for more and more. What is the simple answer to an addiction to salt? **Change your diet.** Eat a lot of fresh fruits, vegetables, and other potassium-rich foods, and eat less salty, processed foods. In my work as a Certified Nutritionist and a weight loss expert, I've encouraged hundreds, if not thousands of people over the past 25 years to change their diets and do just that. Guess what happens? Clients notice after just a few days that their taste buds adjust, and they notice the natural saltiness and sweetness in condiments available to season foods, especially when they eat a wide variety of whole fresh foods including herbs and seasonings. **Put away the saltshaker.** Health officials say no one should eat more than 2,300 milligrams of sodium a day, equal to about a teaspoon of salt (27). People with high blood pressure should eat much less. Just remembering that nearly 75% of the sodium in the typical American diet is in processed foods can help you take skillful action. **Limit, or eliminate, processed and fast foods** from your diet. When you consume them, if you can't eliminate them, make changes at other meals to compensate, choosing whole fresh foods, mostly plants, as a way to balance consumption of processed foods.

Eat a diet rich in potassium containing foods. Remember that potassium is essential to balance sodium intake, and a potassium deficiency can be harmful to your health (28). Potassium deficiency can result in electrolyte imbalances. Recommendations are to eat 4,700 milligrams a day. How to hit these numbers: again, eat sources of potassium-rich foods.

Some of the best sources of potassium are also the most delicious: try a cup of cooked white beans, which provide 561 milligrams per serving. One cup of cooked dark leafy greens, like spinach, provides over 800 milligrams per serving. A baked potato with skin is close to 1,000 milligrams, and even a medium banana provides over 400 milligrams.

HOOKED ON FAT: THE AMERICAN LOVE STORY

Like many people, rats are happy to gorge themselves on tasty, high-fat treats. Bacon, sausage, chocolate, and even cheesecake quickly became favorites of laboratory rats that recently were given access to these human indulgences—so much so that the animals came to depend on high quantities to feel good, like drug users who need to up their intake to get high.

Researchers decided to see if rats' attraction to fat is connected to changes in the brain connected with neurochemical dependency (29). Many pleasurable behaviors—including eating, sex, and drug use—can trigger the release of dopamine, a feel-good neurotransmitter in the brain. This internal chemical reward

Voronin76/Shutterstock.com

increases the likelihood that the associated action will eventually become a habit through positive reinforcement conditioning. If activated by overeating, these neurochemical patterns can make the behavior tough to change. It is one explanation why researchers find most people who are overweight say, "I would like to control my weight and my eating," but they find it very hard to control their food-related behavior.

Even though research shows a connection between overeating and habit-driven behavior, it has been unclear whether extreme overeating starts because of a chemical irregularity in the brain or if the behavior is changing the brain's biochemical makeup. The rat study suggests that both conditions are possible.

To see just how overeating and obesity alters the brain's reward center, they placed stimulating electrodes in the rats' brains to monitor their changing reward levels. Some rats were given only one hour a day to freely feed on tasty, high-fat foods, and others had unlimited access (18 to 23 hours a day). All the rats, including a control group that was given no human food, had open access to water and standard, healthful lab rat chow. Researchers found that the rats with extended access to the high-fat foods ate little to none of their bland healthy rat chow and quickly grew obese—consuming about twice the amount of calories as the control, chow-only group. The researchers also found that even the rats with limited access to the unhealthful food were doing their best to keep up. These subjects managed, on average, to consume 66% of their daily calories over the course of the single hour per day in which they could eat the junk food, *developing a pattern of compulsive binge eating*. Only the obese rats with extended access to the bad food, however, had sharply increasing thresholds for reward levels.

CREATING OVEREATERS: HOW FOOD COMPANIES CONSPIRE TO HURT OUR HEALTH

> "The food industry understands how to construct and develop food for optimal sensory stimulation and pleasure. Hedonics involves five factors: anticipation, visual appeal, aroma, taste and flavor, and texture, and mouthfeel. We now know that this involves activating certain parts of the brain."
> —*Dr. David Kessler,* The End of Overeating

It is no coincidence that so many people are obese, and despite widespread knowledge that it's bad for you, many people continue to crave junk food. Junk food manufacturers know this and they use the science of nutrition to help capitalize on this fact. Food manufacturers work hard to create "feel-good food" made to include just the right combination of the sugar, fat, and salt our limbic brains love.

Magenta/Shutterstock.com

Writers have shared how food companies use manipulation of ingredients to create food that we can't resist (30). There is even terminology to describe this process: words like pillar ingredients describe the key foundations of processed foods: fat, sugar, and salt. Other terms that relate to processed food include bliss point, which refers to the optimal combination and amount of the pillar ingredients; mouth feel, which is how food "feels" inside a consumers' mouth; flavor burst, where salt crystals are altered scientifically to hijack our taste buds, encouraging overeating; and vanishing caloric density, when processed food melts in our mouths so quickly it overrides the normal process of satisfaction and satiety. We lose the signal from the brain to stop eating with certain foods that are high in fat.

David Kessler describes vanishing caloric density as adult baby food.

"It starts with how many chews there are in a bite. If you take a stimulus and you get a sensory hit and it disappears, what do you do immediately next?

You take another bite.

We're eating, in essence, adult baby food. Twenty years ago the average chews per bite was about 20, now it's two or three. The food goes down in a whoosh and it's very stimulating. It's layered and loaded with fat, sugar, and salt. It's as if you have a roller coaster going on in your mouth. You get stimulated, it disappears instantly and you reach for more." (31)

MINDFULNESS AND THE ABILITY TO CHANGE

Awareness is the first step of mindfulness. In any mindfulness practice, we notice how we feel, and without judgment, pay attention to the experience of feelings (32). Experts in overeating and food addiction suggest that **awareness is the first step** in breaking conditioned hypereating (33). It's no surprise this is the first step alcoholics take when beginning the change process. Once you understand that your brain is being activated, you can consider questions like, "how do I cool off the stimulus?" **Step number 2 is developing your own set of rules regarding overeating.** Kessler believes that it is not possible to try to eat a highly palatable food such as French fries, because it is impossible to stop. So, he suggests a rule to not eat them. In managing his personal issues with overeating, this has been a highly effective strategy. Interestingly, I've found the same types of rules work for me, too—there are just many foods I won't eat because of their ability to manipulate and hijack my taste buds. **Step number 3 is create structure around your eating.** Create a plan, know what you're going to eat, when you're going to eat it, and eat with a certain structure so you're not grabbing food constantly throughout the day. This way of creating boundaries is very helpful in controlling overeating. Boundaries and rules keep the brain in check. If I tell myself, "no French fries, ever," then I'm not tempted each time I drive past a fast food restaurant. It ends the dialog and allows me less anxiety, which means less suffering.

Step number 4 is eat in a planned way, which is peaceful. Chaotic eating patterns cause difficulty for our brains. Snacking constantly is simply a response to cues in the environment. If we eat every time we get a cue from the environment, we're eating all the time. Having a planned structure and routine with food settles this habit response to food stimulation, which is everywhere.

Avoid processed and junk food filled with salt, sugar, and fat. When we eat combinations of fat, sugar, and salt, our brain is being so highly activated, our working memories are preoccupied. We then do not sense the sensation of fullness. This creates habitual overeating. Keeping the hyper stimulation of the reward circuits of the brain calm helps to prevent overeating.

Change how you perceive food. If you look at a food item and say, "look how this is loaded and layered with fat, sugar, and salt; that's not my friend,"(34) we can find a way to end overeating. Changing our own emotional appraisal of food is a type of counter-conditioning that works. If we look at comfort foods such as chocolate cake and say "that's going to make me feel better" we only want it more. Changing for us the unchallenged narrative about these foods is a key. If we continuously seek to feel better through overeating highly palatable foods, we ultimately lose.

4 Step MAC Guide

Mindfully
acknowledge
attention
accept
choose

MINDFUL ACTIVITY: LOOKING CLOSELY

Choose a food object of your affection, a fast food that you like or something that comes in a package with a label listing more than 10 ingredients. Sit in a quiet place, with few distractions. Begin by noticing the wrapper. What do you see? Shiny, colorful, noisy—handle the food item in its wrapper, and as you breathe into your body, notice what sensations appear. Perhaps excitement, curiosity, salivation, impatience. Keep breathing, look closer. Is there a trace of a memory, an experience, a feeling from childhood? Be curious as you contemplate the many sensations this familiar food product brings up for you.

Now open the package. Breathe deeply; is there a smell? Can you describe it? Any qualities to the smell: sweet, savory, and subtle? Maybe you notice something else—see if you can describe it.

Break off a small piece of your beloved food product. As you bring the item to your lips, see if you again notice feelings of excitement, impatience, desire, longing. Stop for a bit—breathe—feel—sense beyond habit. What do you feel?

Take the food into your mouth. Slowly chew, many times.

Allow the food to fully dissolve in your mouth. Notice how many bites it takes to dissolve—what does it feel like in the mouth? Notice your anticipation of the swallow. When it comes, imagine the food moving down your esophagus into your stomach. How do you feel? Nourished? Hungry for more? Is it mouth hunger, stomach hunger, or mind hunger? Can you sense the difference between a craving for more from the salty, sugary, or fatty taste?

Journal your reflections here:

_____
_____
_____
_____
_____
_____
_____

Now go onto the Internet and look up the ingredient list for the food you chose. Find either the Nutrition Facts label (if you don't have the original packaging) or the company's website to look up what is in the food. Notice the ingredient list. Any unfamiliar names? What do they mean? Look them up, read what they are. Reflect on your experience. Does knowing what's in the food change the way you feel? Pause. Breathe. Reflect.

We can learn how to become aware of food ingredients and avoid cues that make us overeat. Noticing what ingredients are in processed food, we can shift in our perception of processed foods from a sense of comfort and pleasure to disgust and harm. Through self-education about processed foods and their health risks, we can learn how to understand our biological foibles and weaknesses with curiosity, compassion, and interest. Through the ability to pay attention without judgment, we open the doorway to a life of purposeful food choice and consumption, maximizing our health benefits and leaving a smaller environmental footprint.

A wonderful way to start the day is with a homemade drink that is healthful, easy to prepare, and nutritious. Filled with potassium, its natural sweetness from fruits and vegetables is undeniable. Enjoy with a slice of 100% whole-wheat toast and nut butter for a nutritionally balanced meal.

The Green Goddess Smoothie

Serves 1

Ingredients

1 apple (cut in quarters)

1 pear (cut in quarters)

1 banana (break in two pieces)

Juice of a lemon

1.5–2 cups of water (can substitute plant-based milk)

¼ cup chopped parsley

3 tablespoons fresh mint (chopped)

1–2 handfuls of fresh greens (any variety)

Place all ingredients in a blender. Blend until desired consistency. Enjoy right away, or save ½ of the drink for later in the day.

REFERENCES

1. Ahima, R. S. 2009. "The End of Overeating." *Journal of Clinical Investigation* 119 (10), pp. 2867–2867.
2. Myles, I. A. 2014. "Fast Food Fever: Reviewing the Impacts of the Western Diet on Immunity." *Nutrition Journal* 13, p. 61.
3. Jacob, A. "Processed Food Definition." [Webpage] *SF Gate Healthy Eating.* Available from: http://healthyeating.sfgate.com/processed-food-definition-2074.html.
4. BioMed Central Limited. 2013, March 7. "Processed Meat Linked to Premature Death, Large Study Finds." *ScienceDaily.* [February 27, 2015]. Retrieved from: www.sciencedaily.com/releases/2013/03/130306220950.htm.
5. Centers for Disease Control and Prevention. 2014. "Overweight and Obesity: Adult Obesity Facts." http://www.cdc.gov/obesity/data/adult.html.
6. Fontaine, K. R., and Barofsky, I. 2001. "Obesity and Health-Related Quality of Life." *Obesity Reviews* 2, pp. 173–182. doi: 10.1046/j.1467-789x.2001.00032.x.
7. Malnick, S., and Knobler, H. 2006. "The Medical Complications of Obesity." *QJM,* 99, *pp.* 565–579. doi: http://dx.doi.org/10.1093/qjmed/hcl085.
8. US Department of Health & Human Services. 2014. "NIH Study Finds Extreme Obesity May Shorten Life Expectancy up to 14 Years." *National Institutes of Health.* http://www.nih.gov/news/health/jul2014/nci-08.htm.
9. Kessler, D. 2009. *The End of Overeating: Taking Control of the Insatiable American Appetite.* New York, NY: Rodale.

10. Avena, N., Rada, P., and Hoebel, B. 2008. "Evidence for Sugar Addiction: Behavioral and Neurochemical Effects of Intermittent, Excessive Sugar Intake." *Neuroscience and Biobehavioral Reviews* 32(1), pp. 20–39. doi: 10.1016/j.neubiorev.2007.04.019.

11. Moss, M. 2013. *Salt, Sugar & Fat: How the Food Giants Hooked Us.* New York, NY: Random House.

12. Wilson. 1991 "Carbohydrate Craving, Mood Changes, and Obesity." *Journal of Clinical Psychiatry* 49, pp. 37–39.

13. Colantuoni, C. I., Schwenker, J., McCarthy, J., Rada, P., Ladenheim, B., Cadet, J. L., Schwartz, G. J., Moran, T. H., and Hoebel, B. G. 2001. "Excessive Sugar Intake Alters Binding to Dopamine and Mu-opioid Receptors in the Brain." *Neuroreport* 12(16), pp. 3549–3552.

14. American Heart Association. 2015. "Frequently Asked Questions About Sodium." Available from: https://www.heart.org/HEARTORG/GettingHealthy/NutritionCenter/HealthyEating/Frequently-Asked-Questions-FAQs-About-Sodium_UCM_306840_Article.jsp.

15. Harvard Health. 2009. "Sodium, Salt, and You." Available from: http://www.health.harvard.edu/newsletter_article/sodium-salt-and-you.

16. Morris, M. J., Na, E. S., and Johnson, A. K. 2008. "Salt Craving: The Psychobiology of Pathogenic Sodium Intake." *Physiology & Behavior* 94(5), pp.709–721. doi:10.1016/j.physbeh.2008.04.008.

17. Leshem, M. 2014. "The Human Penchant for Deranged Salt Balance." In *Neurobiology of Body Fluid Homeostasis: Transduction and Integration.* eds. L. A, De Luca, Jr, J. V. Menani, and A. K. Johnson AK. Boca Raton (FL): CRC Press. Chapter 1. Available from: http://www.ncbi.nlm.nih.gov/books/NBK200972/.

18. Mayo Clinic. 1998–2015. "Sodium: How to Tame Your Salt Habit." Available from: http://www.mayoclinic.org/healthy-living/nutrition-and-healthy-eating/in-depth/sodium/art-20045479.

19. Institute of Medicine (US) Committee on Strategies to Reduce Sodium Intake; Henney, J. E., Taylor, C. L., and Boon, C. S., eds. 2010. *Strategies to Reduce Sodium Intake in the United States.* Washington, DC: National Academies Press (US). "3, Taste and Flavor Roles of Sodium in Foods: A Unique Challenge to Reducing Sodium Intake." Available from: http://www.ncbi.nlm.nih.gov/books/NBK50958/.

20. Centers for Disease Control. 2012. "Get the Facts: Sources of Sodium in Your Diet." Available from: http://www.cdc.gov/salt/pdfs/sources_of_sodium.pdf.

21. Huffington Post, Healthy Living. 2011. "Why Your Sodium-Potassium Ratio Is so Important." Available from: http://www.huffingtonpost.com/2011/07/11/potassium-salt-diet-dangers_n_895124.html.

22. Aaron, K. J.1, and Sanders, P. W. 2013. "Role of Dietary Salt and Potassium Intake in Cardiovascular Health and Disease: A Review of the Evidence." *Mayo Clinic Proceedings* 88(9), pp. 987–995. doi: 10.1016/j.mayocp.2013.06.005.

23. CSPI, Nutrition Action Newsletter. 2010. "Salt. Shaving Salt, Saving Lives." Available from: http://www.cspinet.org/nah/articles/salt.html.

24. Centers for Disease Control. 2014. "Nine of 10 American Kids Eat Too Much Salt: CDC." Available from: http://consumer.healthday.com/cardiovascular-health-information-20/dieting-to-control-salt-health-news-191/nine-of-10-american-kids-eat-too-much-salt-cdc-691582.html.

25. Britton, T. "Review: The End of Overeating." [Webpage] *Society for the Anthropology of Food and Nutrition.* [February 27, 2015]. Available from: http://foodanthro.com/book-reviews/review-the-end-of-overeating/.

26. US Food and Drug Administration. 2014. "Sodium in Your Diet: Using the Nutrition Facts Label to Reduce Your Intake." Available from: http://www.fda.gov/Food/ResourcesForYou/Consumers/ucm315393.htm.

27. Lanham-New, S., and Lambert, H. 2012. "Potassium." *Advances in Nutrition* 3, pp. 820–821. doi: 10.3945/an.112.003012.

28. Johnson, P. M., and Kenny, P.J. 2010. "Dopamine D2 Receptors in Addiction-Like Reward Dysfunction and Compulsive Eating in Obese Rats." *Nature Neuroscience* 13, pp. 635–641.

29. Cannon, G. 2013. "The Food System. Ultra Processing. Big Food Bitten." *World Nutrition, Journal of the World Public Health Nutrition Association* 4, p. 3.

30. McFedries, P. 2013. "The Jargon of Junk Food: Manufactured Foods Need Manufactured Words." Available from: http://spectrum.ieee.org/at-work/innovation/the-jargon-of-junk-food.

31. Mieszkowski, K. 2009. "Why We Can't Eat Just One." In Salon.com. Available from: http://www.salon.com/2009/06/18/overeating/.

32. Williams, J. M. G., Russell, I., and Russell, D. 2008. "Mindfulness-Based Cognitive Therapy: Further Issues in Current Evidence and Future Research." *Journal of Consulting and Clinical Psychology* 76(3), pp. 524–529. doi:10.1037/0022-006X.76.3.524.

33. Galanter, M. 1992. "Overcoming Addiction." Available from: https://www.psychologytoday.com/articles/200910/overcoming-addiction.

34. Moss, M. 2013. "The Extraordinary Science of Addictive Junk Food." *The New York Times.* Available from: http://www.nytimes.com/2013/02/24/magazine/the-extraordinary-science-of-junk-food.html.

MINDFUL EATING REFLECTION JOURNAL

1. Acknowledge
Describe your experience; what did you choose to eat?

2. Intentional Attention

Describe what you noticed during your mindful eating practice.

BREATH:	
BODY:	
EMOTIONS:	
THOUGHTS:	
SENSES:	

3. Accept Without Judgment
Describe judgment; acceptance

4. Choose Your Experience
Intention/willingness; new perspective

5. Mindful Meditation/Mindful Eating Experience (Mindful Practice)
What did you notice about your meditation experience this week?

MINDFUL EATING WEEKLY QUIZ

This is a brief snapshot of your mindful eating skills. It is to help you to identify which skills you may want to change or enhance. Circle the best answer. Don't forget to notice what you already do well. After you complete this quiz, write down a mindful eating goal for the week.

Take this quiz each week of the course.

1. I tend to stop eating when I am full				
←				→
All of the time	Most of the time	Occasionally	Sometimes	Almost Never
2. I eat when I am hungry rather than when I feel emotional				
All of the time	Most of the time	Occasionally	Sometimes	Almost Never
3. I try not to "pick" at food				
All of the time	Most of the time	Occasionally	Sometimes	Almost Never
4. I taste each bite before reaching for the next				
All of the time	Most of the time	Occasionally	Sometimes	Almost Never
5. When I eat, I think about how nourishing the food is for my body				
All of the time	Most of the time	Occasionally	Sometimes	Almost Never
6. I am nonjudgmental of myself, my body and when I accidentally overeat				
All of the time	Most of the time	Occasionally	Sometimes	Almost Never
7. I don't multitask while I eat. When I eat, I just eat and focus on the food in front of me				
All of the time	Most of the time	Occasionally	Sometimes	Almost Never
8. I don't have to eat everything on my plate, I can leave what I don't want				
All of the time	Most of the time	Occasionally	Sometimes	Almost Never
9. I tend to eat slowly, chewing each bite				
All of the time	Most of the time	Occasionally	Sometimes	Almost Never
10. I recognize when I slip into mindless eating (zoned out, popping food into my mouth)				
All of the time	Most of the time	Occasionally	Sometimes	Almost Never
List your Mindful Eating Goals: (ex: learn to be more present when I eat, slow down, stop when I'm full)				

Food Marketing to Children: The Socialization of Food Preferences

Faith Boninger and Alex Molnar, *University of Colorado Boulder*

> "Food marketing affects what children want to eat, what they're willing to eat, what they do eat . . . [and] helps to shape what kids think of as food . . . "
> —Margo Wootan, Director of Nutrition Policy at the Center for Science in the Public Interest (1)

When you think about which foods you like, and why you like them, you probably don't think, "Marketing. The foods I like are the ones that have been 'sold' to me since I was a little kid." However, marketing—including marketing to children—plays a huge role in determining people's food preferences, their eating behavior, and their understanding of the roles that food should play in their lives. Food marketing is ubiquitous in modern western culture, and it especially targets children. Chances are very good that it influenced you.

FOLLOW THE MONEY

Food Companies Want to Reach Children to Ensure Many Years of Revenue

Children have their own pocket money to spend, and food items are what they tend to buy (2). They also influence parent purchases: their parents often consult with them about what to buy, and when they don't, they nag them to do so. For years, marketers have encouraged children to pester their parents until the parents succumb to their request (3). More important than immediate purchases, however, is the potential for future purchases. Children have their whole buying lives ahead of them, and child customers become customers for life.

Marketing Works

Despite the protestations of the food industry that their marketing influences only brand preferences, marketing is an important modern cultural factor that influences what children think of as edible and desirable (2). Think about it: in the twenty-first century United States, we like bacon, soda, and Cheetos—not whale blubber or insects, as people do in other cultures, or bean porridge or hoe cakes, as Americans did in the 1600s. And Cheetos would not have even been thought of as "food" in the United States of the 1600s. Here and now, the food industry and its marketing are a major influence on what we consider desirable to eat.

Because marketing to children does, in fact, work (4), food companies spend a fortune both to do it and to protect their legal right to continue to do it. The food and beverage industry is worth $1.5 trillion (5). In 2009, 48 major food corporations in the United States spent a total of $1.79 billion just to market to children and teens ages between 2 and 17 (6). Between 2009 and 2012, food industry organizations spent more than $175 million lobbying the federal government against changes in policy they feared would limit their ability to advertise to children (5).

74   Chapter 6: Food Marketing to Children: The Socialization of Food Preferences

HOW MARKETING INFLUENCES FOOD PREFERENCES AND EATING BEHAVIOR

Heavily Marketed Foods Tend to Be Branded, Processed, and Unhealthy

In the United States, more than 98% of television food commercials seen by children, and 89% of those seen by teens, are for products high in fat, sugar, or sodium (2). The Federal Trade Commission's analysis of the money spent on food marketing to children found the most marketed types of food to be "quick service restaurant food" (including "fast food"), carbonated drinks, high-sugar breakfast cereals, and snack foods, candy, and frozen desserts (in that order).

TABLE 1

48 major national food and beverage corporations spent approximately $1.79 billion marketing to children aged 2–17 in 2009:
• Quick Service Restaurant foods ($714 million)
• Carbonated beverages ($395 million)
• Breakfast cereal ($186 million)
• Snack foods, candy, and frozen desserts ($123 million)
(Federal Trade Commission, 2012).

Marketing Develops Brand Loyalty

The goal of marketing is for consumers to develop, from an early age, an affinity for and loyalty to a brand. For this reason, marketers try to provide children with as many positive associations with the brand as possible—not to convince them in any kind of logical way that the brand is better, but rather to make them feel good about it (2).

And children are, indeed, "branded". Two-year olds recognize brand logos on product packages (7). By preschool, children recognize brands they've seen on television (8). In one study of preschoolers, researchers asked the children to taste food wrapped in McDonald's packaging and the same food wrapped in plain packaging. The children said the food— even the carrots— in McDonald's packaging tasted better (9).

Advertisements Teach Children What Is "Normal"

Although they don't realize it, children learn more from marketing and advertising than just about a brand of food. They also learn social norms—or at least what marketers want them to believe are social norms. Specifically, food ads portray products as tasty, fun, cool, and exciting, thereby instructing children that these are the dimensions according to which they should judge their food. Advertising's focus on the sensory and rewarding aspects of unhealthy foods creates "hedonic hunger", in which people develop thoughts, feelings, and urges about food that are completely separate from any physical hunger (2).

Given this, it is not surprising that marketing encourages eating as a behavior unconnected to nutrition. The majority of advertisements show kids snacking, rather than eating meals, encouraging them to understand that snacking on yummy food anytime and anywhere, because it's fun and cool and you want it, is normal and desirable (2).

Food Companies Lead the Way in Innovative Ways to Reach and Influence Children

Food marketing is ubiquitous. If you watched a morning of children's television, you would find that most of the commercials are for food. In fact, American children see approximately 13 food commercials every day on TV alone (4,700 a year); and teens see even more (16 per day, or 5,900 a year) (3).

But television is far from the only place where children are exposed to food marketing. In what researchers call a "360 degree" marketing strategy, marketers reach them in many other places (10). Children see "product placements" for food products in movies, TV shows, songs, and videogames (2). They attend sports and entertainment events sponsored by food brands; and the marketing they see for toys, games, and movies is co-marketed with food brands (2).

On their computers and cell phones, children play free "advergames" (Remember Millsberry.com? Some current examples are popsicle.com, lunchables.com and goldfishfun.com). It's no wonder the games are free—in reality, they are commercials in which children immerse themselves for hours. The advergames and brand websites that house them use child game-players to further market to their friends by encouraging them to send e-cards and to post about their play on social media (11).

Schools Are an Important Venue for Food Marketing

School is one place you might imagine would be free from marketing. Not so, however. Schools are a desirable venue for marketers. Outside of school, children are a fragmented market—the jock kids are separate from the theater kids who are separate from the geeky kids—and it's hard to reach all of them. Further, the marketing environment outside of schools is cluttered with a lot of different brands. In school, children are gathered together (not fragmented), and they are a captive audience. The marketing environment is also relatively uncluttered.

Even better for marketers is that children are especially susceptible to marketing in school because any marketing that appears there carries the apparent approval of teachers and administration.

Although many different products are marketed in school, food products are the most marketed there. When we interviewed school principals all over the United States, we found that two-thirds of schools nationwide have marketing for foods high in fat and sugar and Foods of Minimal Nutritional Value ("FMNV" are foods that have been defined by the U.S. Department of Agriculture as having virtually no nutritional value, such as soda and hard candy) (12). Another study, of high schools in Maine, found that despite a law forbidding the marketing of FMNV in Maine schools, 85% of the high schools have it (13).

Food Is Marketed in Many Ways in School

Appropriation of space and exclusive agreements. Sometimes food is obviously advertised in schools—on branded scoreboards in the gym or football field, or on branded soup tureens or freezers in the cafeteria. We call this "appropriation of space" because the brand physically takes up school space.

Vending machines are a special type of appropriation of space in that they don't only sell food, but they also serve as lit-up billboards that then dispense smaller ads—in the form of cans or wrappers—that are then dispersed throughout the school. Typically, they are brought into schools as part of an "exclusive agreement" with the school district that allows for only one brand of a particular product category—such as soft drinks—to be sold and marketed there.

Vending machines are such effective advertisements that one district administrator explained to us that although the Pepsi machines in his district's high schools must be turned off during the school day according to state policy, the Pepsi bottling company with which the district has an exclusive agreement maintains them in the schools primarily for their marketing value (14).

Typically, exclusive "pouring rights" contracts like the one mentioned above are signed for at least 10 years. This means that a child would be likely to see the same brand of soft drink—and only that brand—at school for his or her entire academic career. One study of 20 California, CA, high schools found that 19 of them had vending machines, with a total of 276 total vending machines—that's an average of 14 vending machines per school! (15).

Fundraising, sponsored programs, activities, and educational materials. Corporations also market food in schools by helping schools raise money, and by funding programs and activities and providing free educational materials. These are appealing to cash-strapped schools, although research has shown that they actually do not provide much in the way of funds to schools (12).

An example of how a company can market itself to schoolchildren by sponsoring a program is offered by Panda Express, the quick-service Chinese restaurant chain. Panda Express funds the Franklin-Covey *Leader in Me* program in schools around the country (16). Although the *Leader in Me* program is not at all about food—it's a character-development program—when Panda Express adopts a school for the program, marketing for the restaurants comes with it. The school becomes a "Panda Express School". The local restaurant branch sends food and a big panda for the opening event, and all the children are told about the company's contribution to their school and education (17).

Sometimes marketing is not for the product itself, as is the case with Panda Express, but rather for the world-view espoused by the corporation. Energy Balance 101, a resource of the Healthy Weight Commitment Foundation, provides a good example. The Healthy Weight Commitment Foundation describes itself as a "CEO-led effort to reduce obesity," and the materials it offers to schools as part of Energy Balance 101 are consistent with the world-view of its member corporations (the Foundation's Chair is Chairman and Chief Executive Officer of PepsiCo; some of the other corporate members are General Mills [of Millsberry fame], the Kellogg Company, Nestlé, and the Grocery Manufacturers Association). A full list of corporate members can be found at http://www.healthyweightcommit.org/supporters/members/.

In other words, the stated goal behind the lesson plans, resources, and videos that the Foundation offers elementary school teachers through its Energy Balance 101 portal is to teach children about the balance between "energy in" and "energy out" (18). This is the mantra of the food industry: that no food is "bad", that all foods have a place in a balanced diet, and that each individual is responsible for making sure that they engage in enough physical activity to burn up the calories they ingest.

Although we all do need to take responsibility for our health, the food industry's approach relieves itself of responsibility for producing and encouraging children to eat foods high in added sugar, salt, and fat, and transfers that responsibility to the children themselves. Although the industry is certainly entitled to hold a self-interested perspective, when it presents it to children in school, via their teachers, it is no longer presenting it as a perspective but rather promoting it as fact—to be learned just as math or science facts are learned and to be believed because the teacher endorses it.

Digital marketing. Another important way that corporations market food to children in schools brings us full circle back to the "360 degree" marketing strategy's emphasis on reaching children through their technological devices. More and more, schools and teachers encourage students to spend time online. Many schools have incorporated "1:1 programs," in which each student is provided with her own laptop or tablet. Even without an individual computer, students spend a lot of their educational time online. In fact, one researcher told us that Maine elementary school teachers she interviewed reported that their young students spent an average of 3 hours daily on computers (19).

When children spend time online sites, they visit (e.g., dictionary.com) track and record their behavior for the purpose of developing a behavioral profile for use in targeting marketing to them. The behavioral profile is "anonymized", which means that the marketers that buy it don't know any given child's personally identifying information, but they do know her interests based on which sites she visits. Adults' behavior is tracked the same way, of course, but adults are not sent naively into the online seas in the same way that students are by their schools.

Sent online to an educational site, children are likely to wander from it to linked commercial sites. One extremely successful such a site is *My Coke Rewards*. Coca-Cola is the most successful digital marketer in the world, and actively targets at teen and young adult audience (17). Just one indication of Coke's digital success: of 10.6 billion total social media brand impressions generated by the Top

100 brands in July 2012, 1.4 billion were generated by Coca-Cola (not even counting those impressions generated by Sprite, a Coca-Cola brand that came in eighth place. Second-place Apple generated only 719 million impressions) (17).

My Coke Rewards was launched in 2006 and is still active, with 15 brands and the option for participants to donate their points to participating schools. Participants create online accounts at MyCokeRewards .com so that they can enter PIN codes printed on bottle caps and cartons to redeem rewards.

These are specific techniques used to target teens via *My Coke Rewards*: creating immersive environments that keep visitors engaging with the site (i.e., with its participating brands), infiltrating social networks such as Facebook and Twitter, sending news alerts, rewards info, sweepstakes opportunities, bonus points, and other exclusives via location-based and mobile marketing, collecting personal data both from visitors themselves and from others whose profiles suggest that they would be likely to be interested in the program, and studying the subconscious in order to try to trigger it (20).

With each visit to the site, participants supply "demographic and psychographic details" that allow Coke's marketing team to "identify consumers across brands and experiences, and learn when and how to connect with them"—by, for instance, personalizing the look and messaging of a particular web page, email, or mobile content, or by sending an exclusive offer (17).

These strategies are pioneered and mastered by Coca-Cola and other food corporations (e.g., Frito-Lay, McDonald's, PepsiCo), but are used widely by countless companies on the Internet, where encouraging consumer "engagement" with brands is the prime marketing goal (20). Children visit commercial sites on their "own" time, but are also guided to them when they enter the online marketplace for educational purposes.

CLOSING THOUGHTS

It has been said that the food industry is "working from the playbook of the tobacco industry." To some extent this is true: the industry aggressively markets its products and worldview, denies responsibility for the epidemic of metabolic syndrome and obesity, and has funded research that it can point to in countering scientific findings that incriminate its products (21).

However, marketing has leaped forward in its sophistication in the twenty-first century, and food corporations are at its forefront. The industry's active targeting of children is designed to create customers now and in the future by influencing children's developing preferences about food and food brands, their eating behaviors, and their understanding of the role of food and exercise in their lives.

How Mindfulness Can Help

Marketing is so omnipresent in the background of the modern Western lifestyle that most people tend to discount the extent of its influence on them. Knowing that food marketing works, and that it has likely worked on you, can be overwhelming and threatening. A mindful approach to this knowledge can help on several levels.

Activity One: Marketing and You

Take a few moments to reflect on and journal your thoughts about this chapter. Did anything surprise you? Do you notice any feelings about what you've learned? Are you surprised by your response?
Remember to:

1. acknowledge your thoughts and feelings;
2. pay attention to them;
3. accept them without judgment; and
4. make a choice in how you will experience your thoughts and feelings, and how you will act on them.

Being curious and gentle with your experience can be a helpful support for this activity.

Activity Two: Mindful Eating

Food that is marketed as "healthy" is often still processed, and still contains added sugar, fat, and/or salt. Granola is a good example. Why not try making your own, truly healthy granola? Take some unsalted, raw nuts (a mix of pecans, walnuts, and almonds is especially good) and some rolled oats. Spread them out on a cookie sheet and bake them for 10 minutes at 350 degrees, until lightly toasted (oats should be tan-colored and nuts slightly darker than they were before. Check them periodically to make sure they don't burn—if you smell nuts, they're probably burning!). Let them cool.

Try your granola mixed with plain yogurt and some fresh fruit. Berries and bananas are naturally sweet. How does your creation—unbranded, with no added sugar or salt—taste to you? What are your thoughts and feelings in response to this new taste sensation? As you pay attention to them and accept them without judgment, you will be in a position to choose—now and in the future—the food you eat.

REFERENCES

1. Wootan, M. 2012. Interviewed on *The Knife and Fork Show* (Season 1, Episode 1; quotation at 5:07). Available from: http://www.youtube.com/watch?v=STtUmjKfRt4&feature=plcp/.
2. Harris, J. L., Pomeranz, J. L., Lobstein, T., and Brownell, K. 2009. "A Crisis in the Marketplace: How Food Marketing Contributes to Childhood Obesity and What Can be Done." *Annual Review of Public Health* 30, pp. 211–225.
3. Rudd Center. 2013. "Food Marketing to Youth." Available from: http://www.yaleruddcenter.org/what_we_do.aspx?id=4.
4. Institute of Medicine. 2006. *Food Marketing to Children and Youth: Threat or Opportunity?* Washington, DC: The National Academies Press. Available from: http://www.nap.edu/books/0309097134/html/.
5. Wilson, D., and Roberts, J. 2012, April 27. "Special Report: How Washington Went Soft on Childhood Obesity." *Reuters*. Available from: http://www.reuters.com/article/2012/04/27/us-usa-foodlobby-idUSBRE83Q0ED20120427/.

6. Federal Trade Commission. 2012, December. *A Review of Food Marketing to Children and Adolescents: Follow-Up Report.* Washington, DC: Author. Available from: http://www.ftc.gov/os/2012/12/121221 foodmarketingreport.pdf/.

7. Valkenburg, P. M., and Buijzen, M. 2005. "Identifying determinants of Young Children's Brand Awareness: Television, Parents and Peers." *Journal of Applied Developmental Psychology* 26(4), pp. 456–468.

8. Macklin, M. C. 1996. "Preschoolers' Learning of Brand Names from Visual Cues." *Journal of Consumer Research* 23, pp. 251–261.

9. Robinson, T. N., Borzekowski, D. L., Matheson, D. M., and Kraemer, H. C. 2007. "Effects of Fast Food Branding on Young Children's Taste Preferences." *Archives of Pediatric and Adolescent Medicine* 161 (8), pp. 792–797. Available at: http://archpedi.jamanetwork.com/article.aspx?articleid=570933.

10. Chester, J., and Montgomery, K. 2007, May. *Interactive Food and Beverage Marketing: Targeting Children and Youth in the Digital Age.* Berkeley, CA: Public Health Institute. Available from: http://digitalads.org/documents/digiMarketingFull.pdf/.

11. Moore, E. S. 2006, July. "It's Child's Play: Advergaming and the Online Marketing of Food to Children." Kaiser Family Foundation. Available from: https://kaiserfamilyfoundation.files.wordpress.com/2013/01/7536.pdf.

12. Molnar, A., Garcia, D. R., Boninger, F., and Merrill, B. 2006, 1 January. *A National Survey of the Types and Extent of the Marketing of Foods of Minimal Nutritional Value in Schools.* Commercialism in Education Research Unit, Arizona State University. Available from: http://nepc.colorado.edu/publication/national-survey-types-and-extent-marketing-foods-minimal-nutritional-value-schools.

13. Polacsek, M., O'Roarke, K., O'Brien, L., Blum, J. W., and Donahue, S. 2012, March–April. "Examining Compliance with a Statewide Law Banning Junk Food and Beverage Marketing in Maine Schools." *Public Health Reports* 127, pp. 216–223. Available from: http://www.une.edu/news/2012/upload/PHRarticle-Marketing-Polacsek.pdf/.

14. Kuhn, B. 2013, January 15. Personal communication with Faith Boninger (telephone).

15. Craypo, L., Francisco, S. S., Boyle, M., and Samuels, S. 2006. *Food and Beverage Marketing on California High School Campuses Survey: Findings and Recommendations.* California Project Lean. Available from: http://www.californiaprojectlean.org/docuserfiles//SchoolMarketingReport2006.pdf/.

16. FranklinCovey Education. 2015. "Sponsors." Available from: http://www.theleaderinme.org/sponsors/.

17. Molnar, A, Boninger, F., Harris, M. D., Libby, K. M., and Fogarty, J. 2013. *Promoting Consumption at School: Health Threats Associated with Schoolhouse Commercialism—The Fifteenth Annual Report on Schoolhouse Commercializing Trends: 2011–2012.* Boulder, CO: National Education Policy Center. Available from: http://nepc.colorado.edu/publication/schoolhouse-commercialism-2012.

18. Healthy Weight Commitment Foundation. 2014. "K-2 Module 1: Introduction to Energy Balance." Available from: http://www.togethercounts.com/at-school/modules/k-2-module-1-introduction-energy-balance.

19. Polacsek, M. 2014. "Digital Food Marketing." Unpublished raw data.

20. Center for Digital Democracy and Berkeley Media Studies Group. (n.d.). "Case Studies: My Coke." *Interactive Food & Beverage marketing: Targeting Children and Youth in the Digital Age.* Available from: http://digitalads.org/documents/digiMarketingFull.pdf/.

21. Taubes, G., and Couzens, C. K. 2012, December. "Big Sugar's Sweet Little Lies: How the Industry Kept Scientists from Asking: Does Sugar Kill? Mother Jones." Available from: http://www.motherjones.com/environment/2012/10/sugar-industry-lies-campaign.

MINDFUL EATING REFLECTION JOURNAL

1. Acknowledge
Describe your experience; what did you choose to eat?

2. Intentional Attention

Describe what you noticed during your mindful eating practice.

BREATH:	
BODY:	
EMOTIONS:	
THOUGHTS:	
SENSES:	

3. Accept Without Judgment
Describe judgment; acceptance

4. Choose Your Experience
Intention/willingness; new perspective

5. Mindful Meditation/Mindful Eating Experience (Mindful Practice)
What did you notice about your meditation experience this week?

MINDFUL EATING WEEKLY QUIZ

This is a brief snapshot of your mindful eating skills. It is to help you to identify which skills you may want to change or enhance. Circle the best answer. Don't forget to notice what you already do well. After you complete this quiz, write down a mindful eating goal for the week.

Take this quiz each week of the course.

1. I tend to stop eating when I am full				
All of the time	Most of the time	Occasionally	Sometimes	Almost Never
2. I eat when I am hungry rather than when I feel emotional				
All of the time	Most of the time	Occasionally	Sometimes	Almost Never
3. I try not to "pick" at food				
All of the time	Most of the time	Occasionally	Sometimes	Almost Never
4. I taste each bite before reaching for the next				
All of the time	Most of the time	Occasionally	Sometimes	Almost Never
5. When I eat, I think about how nourishing the food is for my body				
All of the time	Most of the time	Occasionally	Sometimes	Almost Never
6. I am nonjudgmental of myself, my body and when I accidentally overeat				
All of the time	Most of the time	Occasionally	Sometimes	Almost Never
7. I don't multitask while I eat. When I eat, I just eat and focus on the food in front of me				
All of the time	Most of the time	Occasionally	Sometimes	Almost Never
8. I don't have to eat everything on my plate, I can leave what I don't want				
All of the time	Most of the time	Occasionally	Sometimes	Almost Never
9. I tend to eat slowly, chewing each bite				
All of the time	Most of the time	Occasionally	Sometimes	Almost Never
10. I recognize when I slip into mindless eating (zoned out, popping food into my mouth)				
All of the time	Most of the time	Occasionally	Sometimes	Almost Never
List your Mindful Eating Goals: (ex: learn to be more present when I eat, slow down, stop when I'm full)				

Sustainable Living, Food Production, and Animal Welfare

Courtesy of Maria Napoli

> *I am mindful of what I eat*
> *Where I purchase my food*
> *Where and how my food is grown*
> *I am determined to give my body and the environment*
> *The respect it deserves today and everyday*
>
> (Napoli)

"We love dogs and eat cows not because dogs and cows are fundamentally different—cows, like dogs, have feelings, preferences, and consciousness—but because our *perception* of them is different" (1).

CHOICE OR HABIT

Have you ever thought about the food choices you make on a daily basis? Eating is a habit-driven activity, and the choices we make are shaped by early exposures to certain foods, belief systems about types of food choices, and cultural practices (2). Many of our habits surrounding food and eating go unexamined throughout our lives, unless a health crisis finds us. We may be forced to intentionally think about changing from eating unhealthy foods such as processed and convenience foods, or foods high in saturated fat (3). We live to eat, unless we are jolted into mindful awareness following the recognition that our lifetime patterns of eating have not served us well.

Why do we eat the foods we do? Biologically we eat in response to hunger. Hunger encourages us to make a food choice. However, hunger in our culture of plenty is not driven by biology (4). Other things drive hunger and the quest to eat including seeing, smelling, reading, or even thinking about food (5). Hearing music can remind us of a good meal, evoking the desire to eat. Walking by a place where you once ate something delicious can do the same. Even after you've just had a big lunch, and you are incredibly full, imagining something delicious can start salivation (6). Being genuinely hungry in the sense of physiologically needing food matters little. Desire to eat is different from biological hunger. We may notice that a walk past a doughnut shop can stimulate something we call "hunger", independent of level of fullness. Studies show that rats that have been filled up with rat food are just as eager to eat chocolate cereal as hungry rats are to eat laboratory chow (7). The human animal is very much the same. More often than not, we eat because *we want* to eat—not because we need to. Recent studies show that our physical level of hunger, in fact, shows little correlation with how much hunger we say that we feel or how much food we go on to eat. Most of the time we are unaware of these forces on our food choices, desires, and timing of when we eat (8).

This is because we are surrounded by food, which is cheap, widely available, delicious and easy to obtain. Along with this nearly unlimited access to tasty food choices is a disconnection from where our food comes from, and we rarely think about the implications of the food choices we make and why we habitually make them (9). Our mindless monster (10) takes over, and we seek out, select, and consume foods that may or may not be healthful, and may actually harm us. We even consume foods that harm the environment (11).

Eating Animals or Eating Plants? Which Is Sustainable?

Consider how common and ordinary it is to eat animal protein in our culture. In the United States, on average, we eat 31 animals per person, each year, or 2,400 animals during an average individual's lifetime (12). This does not include seafood, but does count poultry, which makes up over 95% of the numbers. If we add in fish, we eat the equivalent of about 16 pounds of seafood per year, on top of chicken, cows, and pigs. We eat animals despite of a tremendous body of scientific and nutritional evidence that indicates consuming animal protein is harmful for our health (13), our environment (14), and the planet (15).

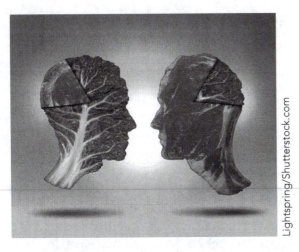

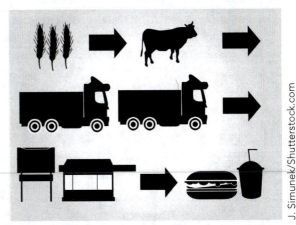

We know from nutrition scientists and environmental experts that eating animals is a leading cause of some of the most serious diseases in the Western world today, including cardiac disease, diabetes, and cancer (14, 15). According to the Academy of Nutrition and Dietetics, eating a plant-based diet is sound nutrition and is more healthful than an animal protein diet (16). In addition to the saturated fat content which animal foods possess, we face other issues with animal foods. Research finds substantial contamination with dangerous chemicals including arsenic, ammonia, and mercury; drugs such as antibiotics and synthetic hormones (which may lead to drug-resistant infections); pesticides; and high levels of fecal matter (17–21).

Far from the idyllic family farm, 99% of the meat, eggs, and dairy that Americans eat come from concentrated animal feeding operations (CAFOs) (22). Not only is eating animal protein harmful to our health and the environment (23), animals are industrially raised for our consumption under extraordinarily inhumane and dangerous conditions. Thinking about eating animals for food goes beyond our own and the environment's health, and takes us, if we awaken to the information, to our own empathy, compassion, and humanity (1).

CAFOs represent the worst in the industrialization and commoditization of the production of animals as food (24). Thousands of animals are crammed together in filthy and unsanitary conditions. Research shows that CAFOs are a leading cause of pandemic flus, avian influenza, mad cow disease, and deadly food-borne illnesses such as *E. coli*, salmonella, and listeria (24).

Here are some facts about confined animal operations (23, 24):

- Animals that are raised in industrial conditions to be consumed live and die in misery. They are born into gigantic, filthy, overcrowded, windowless factories. Taken away from their mothers shortly after birth, they are castrated, debeaked, dehorned, and branded without anesthesia. Female cows are kept pregnant continuously and are forcibly impregnated over and over in a process where they are confined and unable to lay down or turn around. When they are no longer productive, they are slaughtered.
- Animal slaughter takes place in relentless disassembly lines. It is not uncommon for animals to be conscious while slaughtered, since the pace of the line makes errors in stunning animals (knocking them unconscious prior to slitting their throats) common. Animals are hung, shackled, and bled while fully conscious, and sometimes boiled alive. Nearly every animal-based meal comes from a sentient being, who lived and died in agony.

- According to the United Nations, animal agriculture is a significant contributor to some of the biggest environmental problems facing the twenty first century, including water pollution, deforestation, erosion, species extinction, oceanic biodiversity destruction, greenhouse gas emissions, fresh water depletion, and chemical wastes (25).

One Harvard educated psychologist, Dr. Melanie Joy, writes about the emotional costs from eating animals. She notes that in order to eat the flesh or secretions (eggs/milk) of a once-living being, we need to disconnect, psychologically and emotionally, from the truth of our experience.

"We need to numb our authentic thoughts and emotions to block our awareness and our empathy for the animal who became our food—and awareness and empathy are integral to our sense of self" (26).

Take a pause for a mindful moment. What do you notice as you contemplate your own practices and beliefs about animal protein? Notice your body. Do you feel tightness, tension, or other holding? Notice your breath. Breathe into any tightness or tension you feel, allowing your body to soften and expand. Notice your judgments. Allow thoughts to come and go like clouds floating through the sky. Go deeper. Do you sense any emotions, such as sadness, sorrow, or compassion? Allow the feelings of compassion toward yourself, as you courageously face your own beliefs, practices, and habits regarding the food you eat.

When we wake up and allow ourselves to see eating animals through an emotional lens, it becomes clear that we are only able to participate if we are "mindless" and unaware of what the life of a factory-farmed animal is like. This may be one explanation for why we often do not want to know, or hear about animal welfare. It is another reason why food producers don't want us to know, and hide the truth of factory farming from us. It is too painful and disturbing.

Psychologists call this "cognitive dissonance". According to Festinger (27), when we confront a situation that involves conflicting attitudes, beliefs, or behaviors, we experience a feeling of discomfort leading to an alteration in one of the attitudes, beliefs, or behaviors in order to reduce the discomfort and restore balance. Our motives are powerful toward consistency, and because of this we may engage in irrational and sometimes maladaptive behavior. Instead of examining our behaviors and potentially changing them, we reduce our dissonance, reducing tension, by adjusting our thoughts to allow for the maladaptive behavior. This returns us to homeostasis, as our thoughts and emotions remain unexamined. Perhaps, this is a consequence of not critically or compassionately examining our thoughts and behaviors. Perhaps, it is an explanation for mindless behavior. Festinger would suggest that our psychological orientation simply obtains agreement in order to proceed with our potentially disappointing or unhealthful behaviors. We adjust our thoughts in order to proceed with our desired actions, all at the level of the subconscious.

Ignorance is bliss.

As a spiritual family and a human family, we can all help avert climate change with the practice of mindful eating. Going vegetarian may be the most effective way to stop climate change.

Being vegetarian is already enough to save the world.

—from Thich Nhat Hanh's 2007 "Blue Cliff Letter" (28)

Lukatme/Shutterstock.com

Leremy/Shutterstock.com

This perspective provides a mindful way to approach the decision that can be framed as a choice, to eat animals or to choose to abstain from eating animals. Some choose, instead, to eat a whole foods, plant-based diet. Many of us have never considered how we eat to be a choice; we simply eat the same or similar foods of our childhood, communities, and cultural roots.

> "By most measures, confined animal production systems in common use today fall short of current ethical and societal standards."—Pew Commission on Industrial Farm Animal Production

What is the true price we pay in order to consume a cheap hamburger? (29). The giant corporations who have industrialized the processing of animal protein work tirelessly to conceal the release of any information regarding how meat, chicken, turkey, and pork products are made in the United States. We only know what we do about animal welfare thanks to heroic efforts of activists and journalists who go undercover in CAFOs. Corporate interests are trying harder than ever to prevent *any* information on how our meat is produced to reach consumers. They've even taken legal steps to silence anyone who tries to reveal the truth about where our food comes from. Called "Ag-Gag" laws (30), anti-whistleblower bills seek to criminalize whistleblowing on factory farms, keeping consumers in the dark about where their food is coming from. Despite the fact that whistleblowing has played a vital role in exposing animal abuse, unsafe working conditions, and environmental problems on industrial farms, the agribusiness industry-written anti-whistleblower laws effectively block anyone from exposing animal cruelty, food-safety issues, poor working conditions, and more in factory farms. These bills could do this by:

- Banning taking a photo or video of a factory farm without permission,
- Essentially making it a crime for an investigator to get work at a factory farm, or
- Requiring mandatory reporting with impossibly short timelines so that no pattern of abuse can be documented.

In 2013, 15 anti-whistleblower bills were introduced in 11 states: Arkansas, California, Indiana, Nebraska, New Hampshire, New Mexico, North Carolina, Pennsylvania, Tennessee, Wyoming, and Vermont. So far, none have passed.

SUSTAINABLE LIVING MINDFULLY EATING: A SOLUTION?

In order to make conscious choices, we embrace mindfulness as a practice to help us be awake, aware, and alive. How might we mindfully frame a philosophy of eating that aligns with our developing mindful awareness?

Eat Conscientiously

Since nearly all the animal products available in supermarkets and restaurants (meat, seafood, eggs, and dairy) come from factory farms or destructive, inhumane fishing methods, we may wish to examine our own beliefs and values to see if we wish to revisit the unquestioned and unexamined practice of eating animals.

The Foods We Eat

The egg and chicken industries are among the most abusive to animals (31). In light of this, some conscious eaters choose to eat beef, but boycott poultry and eggs. Some skip eating meat when eating out, but at home where there is more control eat as a selective omnivore. Some choose to eliminate animal products out of their diets entirely.

Labels

The mindful consumer can, with care, selectively eat products from animals raised outside the factory system. This is thanks to labeling laws, however, most labels are misleading or meaningless. Those who are interested in labels that are accurate as opposed to advertisements need to review labeling guides from reputable sources (32). Here is a condensed guide to the most commonly used terms you may find on animal products:

Certified Organic	The animals must be allowed outdoor access, with ruminants (cows, sheep, and goats) given access to pasture. Amount of outdoor time is undefined. Animals must be provided with bedding materials. Use of hormones, antibiotics prohibited. Surgical procedures (e.g., castration) are permitted without anesthesia. Compliance verified through third-party auditing; requirements through USDA's National Organic Program (33).
Free Range Chickens, Turkeys	Birds "should" have outdoor access. No requirements on stocking density, frequency or duration of outdoor access, nor quality of the land accessible to the animals is defined. Surgical procedures without pain relief allowed. Producers submit affidavits to the U.S. Department of Agriculture that support animal production claims in order to receive labeling approval.
Grass Fed	Ruminant animals fed a diet solely of grass and forage, with the exception of milk fed before weaning. Animals have access to the outdoors and can engage in some natural behaviors like grazing. Must have continuous pasture access during growing season. Surgery without anesthesia permitted. Producers submit affidavit to USDA supporting their animal production claims in order to receive approval to use the label.

Cage Free	Unlike birds raised for eggs, those raised for meat are rarely caged prior to transport. As such, this label on poultry products has virtually no relevance to animal welfare. However, the label is helpful when found on egg cartons, as most egg-laying hens are kept in severely restrictive cages prohibiting most natural behavior, including spreading their wings.
Certified Humane	Must keep animals in conditions that allow for exercise and freedom of movement. Crates, cages, and tethers are prohibited. Outdoor access is not required for poultry or pigs, but is required for other species. Stocking densities are specified to prevent the overcrowding of animals. All animals must be provided with bedding materials. Hormone and non-therapeutic antibiotic use is prohibited. Pain relief must be used for physical alterations (castration and disbudding) for cattle. For other mammals, anesthesia and analgesia must be used over 7 days of age, but not earlier. Poultry may have parts of their beaks removed without painkillers, though not after 10 days of age. The program also covers slaughter methods. Compliance is verified through auditing by the labeling program. Certified Humane is a program of Humane Farm Animal Care (34).
5-Step Animal Welfare Rating System	Animals rated according to different levels of welfare standards, from Step 1 to Step 5+. Program is audited and certified by independent third parties. Step 1: no cages/crates; Step 2: environmental enrichment for indoor production systems; Step 3: outdoor access; Step 4: pasture-based production; Step 5: animal-centric approach with all physical alterations prohibited; Step 5+: entire life of animal spent on same integrated farm, all transport disallowed. Hormone, sub-therapeutic antibiotic use is prohibited (35).
Hormone Free, rBGH Free, rBST Free, and No Hormones Added	These labels on dairy products mean the cows were not given with rBGH or rBST, genetically engineered hormones that increase milk production. Hormones are commonly used to speed growth in beef production, and their use by both the beef and dairy industries are associated with animal welfare problems (31). Chicken and pig producers are not legally allowed to use hormones. These claims do not have significant relevance to the animals' living conditions. Painful surgical procedures without any pain relief are permitted. There may be some verification of this claim, but not necessarily.

Where We Shop

Never underestimate the power of the purchaser to drive changes. Where you shop can make a difference. Progressive independent grocers or the Whole Foods chain of supermarkets (who have driven tremendous changes in labeling of humanely treated animals) (36, 37) tend to source many of their animal products from local producers or operations with higher animal welfare and sustainability standards. Too expensive to purchase sustainably raised meat? Commit to one meal a week of humane meat, or switch a meal to a plant-based one. Notice how you feel when you make this change with only one step forward. If you notice a difference, physically, mentally, or emotionally, make another. Explore local farmers markets or food coops, too, as alternatives to your traditional shopping patterns.

SIGNS OF POSITIVE CHANGE

There is a revolution happening on our plates! Not only does what we purchase matter, and where we buy our food, but also significant are the political changes that improve standards for farms. Pending state and federal legislation may improve conditions for farm animals (32). Other legislation addresses the effects of farms on our environment (37) and communities (38).

Political action matters, too. Tell Congress that you want to support alternatives to factory farming (39). Talk with the people who produce your food. Ask them to tell you where your food comes from. If you aren't allowed to see where it originates, you might reconsider whether you should eat it. Stay informed on current issues regarding more humane and sustainable farming. Two great sources are Farm Forward (39) and the Humane Society of the United States (32).

Here is a short list of some of the organizations advocating for a change in Sustainable Living and Mindful Eating:

- Farm Forward—www.farmforward.com
- Farm Sanctuary—www.farmsanctuary.org
- Food and Water Watch—www.foodandwaterwatch.org
- Food Democracy Now!—www.fooddemocracynow.org
- Humane Society of the United States—www.hsus.org
- People for the Ethical Treatment of Animals—www.peta.org
- Sierra Club—www.sierraclub.org
- Sustainable Table—www.sustainabletable.org
- Waterkeeper Alliance—www.waterkeeperalliance.org

"So tenacious can our habits of life and mind be that even today, despite everything we know and the genuine alternatives we have for a nutritious diet, less than 1 percent of U.S. adults have turned away from factory-farmed meat for ethical reasons" (40).

Krasimira Nevenova/Shutterstock.com

As humans, we possess an incredible capacity to look the other way when things are inconvenient or dissonant. In one respect, it is part of our humanness. Ancient wisdom might suggest that looking the other way is a hindrance to mindfulness. Any time we allow our awareness to rest in the past or the future and away from the present moment, we miss out on only what we are guaranteed, this very moment. A mindfulness practice offers us the capacity to change, by examining with curiosity, compassion, and kindness our habits of mind and body. We can notice how we feel when we look at the ways we habitually act, and in so doing; can choose to intentionally take more skillful action. Habits of life and mind are tenacious. So are hindrances to mindfulness. Hindrances cloud the clear water of awareness, and keep us from moving toward insight. As we develop compassion toward others, we develop compassion for ourselves, and for all living things. From a mindfulness perspective, every action (speech, thought, and behavior) has a result or subsequent reaction. Wholesome actions will cause results or effects, and unwholesome acts will cause results and effects. It is up to each one of us to decide for ourselves whether the actions we take are wholesome or unwholesome. As we develop a greater sense of inner and outer awareness fostered through our mindfulness practice, we can recognize our synergistic connection to all living things (41). With greater awareness, comes greater responsibility. As you approach your own mindfulness practice, with gentleness and curiosity, you may find yourself changing habits in ways that provide excitement and surprise.

Even eating one plant-based meal a week can make a difference. It's not necessary to give up eating meat; experiment with easy, delicious, and satisfying ways to try plant-based meals. Shifting gently can be easy and delicious. Try this excellent veggie burger with a bite that will make you forget about beef!

Buckwheat Burgers with Sesame Gravy

Ingredients

1 cup cooked buckwheat

½-teaspoon thyme

1½ cups cooked garbonzo beans

½-cup sourdough breadcrumbs

1 stalk celery, minced fine

1 green onion, sliced

½-teaspoon marjoram

2 tablespoons finely minced parsley

1-teaspoon tamari soy sauce

Approximately ½-cup water

½-teaspoon sesame oil

Mash the beans until smooth. Add all the other ingredients, and just enough water to moisten so the mixture is stiff and not too sticky. Shape into slightly flattened patties. Bake on an oiled cookie sheet at 375°F for 25 minutes, or until the top is a little crispy. Serve with sesame gravy.

Sesame Gravy

Ingredients

1 cup water

1 heaping tablespoon kuzu*

3-tablespoon sesame seeds

2–3 teaspoons tamari soy sauce

Roast the seeds by stirring in a skillet over medium heat until they smell nutty and crumble easily between thumb and forefinger. Grind into butter in the blender or suribachi. Dissolve kuzu in cool water, then combine all ingredients and heat. Stir until it thickens.

Kuzu is a natural thickening agent you can use to give the gravy a nice texture and consistency. Made from a plant that is common in the South, it is a starch that is commonly used as a food ingredient. In some countries, it is dissolved as a beverage. It is an alkaline food, and in ancient traditions was used for treating digestive issues.

REFERENCES

1. Joy, M. 2010 *Why We Love Dogs, Eat Pigs, and Wear Cows: An Introduction to Carnism: The Belief System That Enables Us to Eat Some Animals and Not Others.* Newburyport, MA: Conari Press.
2. Meiselman, H. J. H. ed. 1996. *Food Choice, Acceptance and Consumption.* London: Boundary Row.
3. HBO Films. 2013. "The Weight of The Nation: Confronting America's Obesity Epidemic." Available from: http://theweightofthenation.hbo.com/films/main-films/Consequences.
4. ABC News. 2009. "Is Hunger Biological or Is It Just in My Head, and Is There Anything I Can Do to Control It?" [Retrieved February 18, 2015]. Available from: http://abcnews.go.com/Health/WellnessResource/story?id=6763530.
5. Sharp Brains. 2007. "Judith Beck: Train Your Brain to Think Like a Thin Person." [Retrieved February 18, 2015]. Available from: http://sharpbrains.com/blog/2007/09/17/judith-beck-train-your-brain-to-think-like-a-thin-person/.
6. Blackman, M., and Kvaska, C. 2011. *Nutrition Psychology: Improving Dietary Adherence.* Sudbury, MA: Jones and Bartlett.
7. Konnikova, M. 2014. "Why Do We Eat, and Why Do We Gain Weight?" [Webpage]. *The New Yorker*, April 9. Available from: http://www.newyorker.com/science/maria-konnikova/why-do-we-eat-and-why-do-we-gain-weight.
8. The European Food Information Council. 2015. "The Determinants of Food Choice." [Webpage] *EUFIC.org.* [February 15, 2015]. Available from: http://www.eufic.org/.
9. Slow Movement. 2015. "What Are Community Food Systems?" [February 19, 2015]. Available from: http://www.slowmovement.com/cfs.php.
10. Napoli, M. 2011. *Tools for Mindful Living: Steppingstones for Practice.* Dubuque, IA: Kendall Hunt.
11. Walsh, B. 2013. "The Triple Whopper Environmental Impact of Global Meat Production." [Webpage]. *TIME Magazine.* [February 19, 2015]. Available from http://science.time.com/2013/12/16/the-triple-whopper-environmental-impact-of-global-meat-production/.
12. The Economist Online. 2013. "Kings of the Carnivores." [Webpage]. *The Economist.* [February 19, 2015]. Available from: http://www.economist.com/blogs/graphicdetail/2012/04/daily-chart-17.
13. Levine, M. E., Suarez, J. A., Brandhorst, S., Balasubramanian, P., Cheng, C.-W., Madia, F., Fontana, L., Mirisola, M. G., Guevara-Aguirre, J., Wan, J., Passarino, G., Kennedy, B. K., Wei, M., Cohen, P., Crimmins, E. M., and Longo, V. D. 2014. "Low Protein Intake Is Associated with a Major Reduction in IGF-1, Cancer, and Overall Mortality in the 65 and Younger but not Older Population." *Cell Metabolism* 19, pp. 407–417.
14. Brooks, C. "Consequences of Increased Global Meat Consumption on the Global Environment—Trade in Virtual Water, Energy & Nutrients." [Webpage]. *Stanford WOODS Institute for the Environment.* [February 15, 2015]. Available from: https://woods.stanford.edu/environmental-venture-projects/consequences-increased-global-meat-consumption-global-environment.
15. Kunzig, R. 2015. "Carnivore's Dilemma." [Webpage]. *National Geographic*, February. [February 15, 2015]. Available from: http://www.nationalgeographic.com/foodfeatures/meat/.
16. Caspero, A. 2014. "Building a Healthy Vegetarian Meal: Myths and Facts." [Webpage]. *Academy of Nutrition and Dietetics*, January 28. [February 10, 2015]. Available from: http://www.eatright.org/resource/food/nutrition/vegetarian-and-special-diets/building-a-healthy-vegetarian-meal-myths-and-facts.
17. Campbell, T. 2005. *The China Study.* Dallas, TX: Benbella Books.
18. Philpott, T. 2010. "USDA Inspector General: Meat Supply Routinely Tainted with Harmful Residues." [Webpage]. *Grist*, April 16. [February 10, 2015]. Available from: http://grist.org/article/2010-04-15-usda-inspector-meat-supply-routinely-tainted-with-harmful-residu/.
19. Pirello, C. 2010. "Is the Early Onset of Puberty in Young Girls Linked to Meat?" [Webpage]. *Huffington Post Health*, August 13. [January 2, 2015]. Available from: http://www.huffingtonpost.com/christina-pirello/is-the-early-onset-of-pub_b_677424.html.
20. Couric, K. 2010. "Animal Antibiotic Overuse Hurting Humans?" [Webpage]. *CBS News*, February 9. [January 10, 2015]. Available from: http://www.cbsnews.com/news/animal-antibiotic-overuse-hurting-humans/.
21. Eisler, P. 2010. "Growing Concern Over Marketing Tainted Beef." [Webpage]. *USA Today*, April 15. [January 15, 2015]. Available from: http://usatoday30.usatoday.com/news/washington/2010-04-12-tainted-meat_N.htm.

22. PBS. 1995–2014. "Frontline: Modern Meat." [Webpage]. *PBS.org.* [January 5, 2015]. Available from: http://www.pbs.org/wgbh/pages/frontline/shows/meat/interviews/schlosser.html.

23. Jowit, J. 2008. "UN Says Eat Less Meat to Curb Global Warming." [Webpage]. *The Guardian*, September 7. Available from: http://www.guardian.co.uk/environment/2008/sep/07/food.foodanddrink.

24. Factory Farming. 2010–2015. "Zoonotic Diseases: The Animal Factory Crucible." [Webpage]. *Factory-farming.com.* [January 5, 2015]. Available from: http://www.factory-farming.com/zoonotic_diseases.html.

25. United Nations. 2010. "UN Report—Meat Free Diet." [Webpage]. *The Guardian UK*, June 2. [February 15, 2015]. Available from: http://www.theguardian.com/environment/2010/jun/02/un-report-meat-free-diet.

26. Joy, M. 2010. *Why We Love Dogs, Eat Pigs, and Wear Cows: An Introduction to Carnism.* San Francisco: Conari Press.

27. Festinger, L. 1957. *A Theory of Cognitive Dissonance.* Stanford: Stanford University Press.

28. Hanh, T. N. 2007. "Blue Cliff Letter." [February 19, 2015]. Available from: http://plumvillage.org/news/new-contemplations-before-eating/.

29. Soloratoff, P. 2013. "In the Belly of the Beast: The Price We Pay for a Cheap Hamburger." [Webpage]. *Rolling Stone Magazine.* [February 22, 2015]. Available from: http://www.rollingstone.com/feature/belly-beast-meat-factory-farms-animal-activists.

30. Carlson, C. 2012. "The Ag Gag Laws: Hiding Factory Farm Abuses from Public Scrutiny." [Website]. *The Atlantic.com.* [February 22, 2015]. Available from: http://www.theatlantic.com/health/archive/2012/03/the-ag-gag-laws-hiding-factory-farm-abuses-from-public-scrutiny/254674/.

31. ASPCA. 2015. "Fight Cruelty: Birds on Factory Farms." [Webpage]. [February 19, 2015]. Available from: https://www.aspca.org/fight-cruelty/farm-animal-cruelty/birds-factory-farms.

32. The Humane Society of the United States. 2012. "How to Read Meat and Dairy Labels." [Webpage]. [February 22, 2015]. Available from: http://www.humanesociety.org/issues/confinement_farm/facts/meat_dairy_labels.html?credit=web_id208408797.

33. USDA. 2014. "National Organic Program." [February 19, 2015]. Available from: http://www.ams.usda.gov/AMSv1.0/nop.

34. Humane Farm Animal Care. 2015. "Certified Humane." [February 19, 2015]. Available from: http://certifiedhumane.org/.

35. Global Animal Partnership. 2015. "For Consumers." [February 19, 2015]. Available from: http://www.globalanimalpartnership.org/for-consumers/.

36. Sustainable Table. 2015. "Food Program." [February 22, 2015]. Available from: http://www.sustainabletable.org/940/food-issues.

37. Food Democracy Now! 2014. "End the Factory Farm Bailout." [February 22, 2015]. Available from: http://fdn.actionkit.com/cms/sign/Factory_Farm_Bailout/#1.

38. Grace. "Sustainable Table." [February 19, 2015]. Available from: http://www.eatwellguide.org/i.php?pd=Home.

39. "Eat." Farm Forward.com. Available from: https://farmforward.com/category/eat/.

40. Arora, N. 2013. "On Eating Animals." The Humanist.com. [February 22, 2015]. Available from: http://thehumanist.com/july-august-2013/on-eating-animals/.

41. Kabat-Zinn, J. 2005. *Coming to Our Senses: Healing Ourselves and the World Through Mindfulness.* New York: NY: Hyperion.

MINDFUL EATING REFLECTION JOURNAL

1. Acknowledge
Describe your experience; what did you choose to eat?

2. Intentional Attention

Describe what you noticed during your mindful eating practice.

BREATH:	
BODY:	
EMOTIONS:	
THOUGHTS:	
SENSES:	

3. Accept Without Judgment
Describe judgment; acceptance

4. Choose Your Experience
Intention/willingness; new perspective

5. Mindful Meditation/Mindful Eating Experience (Mindful Practice)
What did you notice about your meditation experience this week?

MINDFUL EATING WEEKLY QUIZ

This is a brief snapshot of your mindful eating skills. It is to help you to identify which skills you may want to change or enhance. Circle the best answer. Don't forget to notice what you already do well. After you complete this quiz, write down a mindful eating goal for the week.

Take this quiz each week of the course.

1. I tend to stop eating when I am full				
All of the time	Most of the time	Occasionally	Sometimes	Almost Never
2. I eat when I am hungry rather than when I feel emotional				
All of the time	Most of the time	Occasionally	Sometimes	Almost Never
3. I try not to "pick" at food				
All of the time	Most of the time	Occasionally	Sometimes	Almost Never
4. I taste each bite before reaching for the next				
All of the time	Most of the time	Occasionally	Sometimes	Almost Never
5. When I eat, I think about how nourishing the food is for my body				
All of the time	Most of the time	Occasionally	Sometimes	Almost Never
6. I am nonjudgmental of myself, my body and when I accidentally overeat				
All of the time	Most of the time	Occasionally	Sometimes	Almost Never
7. I don't multitask while I eat. When I eat, I just eat and focus on the food in front of me				
All of the time	Most of the time	Occasionally	Sometimes	Almost Never
8. I don't have to eat everything on my plate, I can leave what I don't want				
All of the time	Most of the time	Occasionally	Sometimes	Almost Never
9. I tend to eat slowly, chewing each bite				
All of the time	Most of the time	Occasionally	Sometimes	Almost Never
10. I recognize when I slip into mindless eating (zoned out, popping food into my mouth)				
All of the time	Most of the time	Occasionally	Sometimes	Almost Never
List your Mindful Eating Goals: (ex: learn to be more present when I eat, slow down, stop when I'm full)				

Food and the Environment

Courtesy of Maria Napoli

Enveloped in the blue skies
Drenched in the warm sun
Feet walking softly on the cool grass
I am reminded of our miraculous earth
Showering me with nourishment

(Napoli)

"Whatever we do to the earth, we do to ourselves" (1).
—*Chief Seattle*

Danilo Sanino/Shutterstock.com

D.S. Fractal/Shutterstock.com

Family farms were once diverse, growing hay, oats, corn, and featuring a woodlot and numerous fencerows. Many plants and animals found home here, but since they no longer can, local populations of migratory songbirds and other species are declining. When we think of how and where our food is grown, we often fantasize about something that looks in our minds like a family farm, yet this is no longer the reality. What is a family farm? The truth is there is no hard-and-fast definition. The U.S. Department of Agriculture (USDA) considers a "family farm" any farm where the majority of the business is owned by the operator and his or her relatives; that is, *by a family* (2). The family part is essential, yes, but many experts emphasize the importance of the family being able to exercise true *ownership* and *control* over the business and production decisions made on their farms.

The means of production of food in the United States has become more efficient and more effective as the ownership of farms has shifted. More efficient and effective means that the amount of food produced in the United States has increased and the cost to consumer has significantly declined.

We have moved to an industrialized food production system, and the ownership of the agricultural system has changed dramatically from hundreds of thousands of individual family farmers to a corporate-controlled industrial model. Over time, this shift has impacted rural communities. With lost livelihoods, food production has become anonymous and faceless. This disconnection from how our food is grown is one consequence. Another may be lifestyle-related diseases due to the overconsumption of cheap, highly processed foods. Finally, large-scale corporate farming methods are eroding our soil and polluting our environment (3).

Momente/Shutterstock.com

CORPORATE CONCENTRATION IN AGRICULTURE: WHY IT MATTERS

In a healthy supply and demand economy, multiple companies can sell their goods to multiple buyers in an open, competitive market. But this isn't the case in agriculture, where most farmers are forced to buy their supplies such as seeds, equipment, and fertilizer from just a handful of companies and have very few places to market their goods. The term *corporate concentration* describes the control that a small number of corporations have over food production, distribution, marketing, and consumption through their share of the marketplace (4).

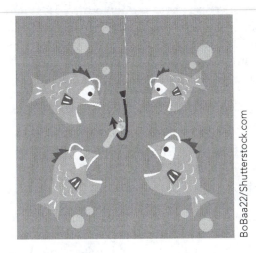

How Concentrated Is It?

The U.S. agricultural sector shows abnormally high levels of concentration. Most economic sectors have concentration ratios around 40%, meaning that the top four firms in the industry control 40% of the market. If the concentration ratio is above 40%, experts believe competition can be threatened and market abuses are more likely to occur: the higher the number, the bigger the threat (4).

The Shocking Naked Truth

Here are the concentration ratios in the agricultural sector:

- Four companies own 83.5% of the beef market (5).
- The top four firms own 66% of the hog industry (6).
- The top four firms control 58.5% of the broiler chicken industry (6).
- In the seed industry, four companies control 50% of the proprietary seed market and 43% of the commercial seed market *worldwide* (7).
- When it comes to genetically engineered (GE) crops, just one company, Monsanto, boasts control of over 85% of U.S. corn acreage and 91% of U.S. soybean acreage (8).

Farms of today are much more likely to be huge operations that produce our food. What are the consequences of this concentration? We've heard about genetically modified crops (GMOs), where seeds are altered before planting to make them pest resistant or fertilizer ready, as two examples. This allows mass production of food such as wheat, corn, and soybeans.

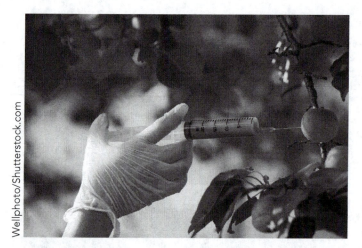

Wellphoto/Shutterstock.com

Other consequences include declining quality (9), obesity and diabetes (10), antibiotics in our food supply (11), and an inefficient meat-centric diet which can only feed 4 million people, compared to the 10 billion who could be fed with a plant-based diet (12). Less talked about are other more serious threats.

Today's farms threaten aquatic systems, because they use enormous amounts of fertilizer to increase corn and soybean yields, and the leached chemicals find their way into our rivers and streams; because the livestock production system relies on confined animal feeding operations (CAFOs), we have unprecedented concentrations of waste and the health challenge of disposing of it (12).

This chapter began with a quote from Chief Seattle reminding us that damaging the Earth ultimately destroys ourselves. T. Colin Campbell in his book *Whole* (13) reminds us that the reverse of this is true: what we do to ourselves damages the Earth. It is not enough to blame the industrialized food system when we consider our own eating habits. Instead, our insatiable demand for inexpensive food has begun to destroy the environment. Rather than thinking that eating one type of food (meat) is "bad" and another type (plants) is "good", consider whether there are consequences to a meat-centric diet. We've discussed some of the health consequences; let's consider some of the environmental consequences. For example, producing animal-based food requires tremendous amounts of resources with environmental destruction a side effect. Cornell University's Dr. David Pimentel has documented the many ways that animal livestock production wastes precious resources. His findings include (14) the following:

- Animal protein production requires eight times as much fossil fuel as plant protein.
- Livestock in the U.S. consumes five times as much grain as the country's entire human population. (*Note*: livestock's natural food is grass, not the corn and soybeans it is routinely fed to fatten it up quickly).
- Each kilogram (equivalent to 2.2 pounds) of beef requires 100,000 liters of water to produce. As a comparison, a kilogram of wheat requires 900 liters, and a kilogram of potatoes, 500 liters.
- Experts concluded in 2006 that 80% of deforestation in the tropics is attributable to the creation of new farmland, the majority of which is used for livestock grazing and feed.

Alan Poulson Photography/Shutterstock.com

All of these problems are ultimately caused by what some call the insatiable demand for an animal protein diet (15). This system of industrialized production of animal protein is unsustainable, damaging, inefficient, and unkind to the planet. This is independent of any detrimental health effects of an animal protein heavy diet, which is scientifically implicated in many, if not most, of the diseases we face today (16). We're using up our natural resources, such as soil and water, faster than we can replenish them. The side effects of producing animal protein in CAFOs include environmental toxins and poisoning the air we breathe (17). We can use our mindfulness practice as a way to look deeper, without judgment, to find skillful solutions and *respond*, rather than *react* to this information (18).

MINDFULNESS AND THE FOOD SYSTEM: A SUSTAINABLE MODEL

A challenge when looking at the food system in the United States is the overwhelming nature of the information about how our food is produced. At nearly every turn, one can be consumed by videos and images of the way our food gets onto our plate. The nature of animal welfare is shocking (see Chapter 7), and covertly recorded videos documenting animal abuse at the hands of factory farmers are heartbreaking. In researching this book, I found it incredibly difficult to stay engaged. My heart was broken open by the images of tortured animals, all in the name of a mass-produced hamburger or hotdog. It was depressing and upsetting to learn the environmental costs due to the industrialization of our food supply. According to a report published in 2007 by the Food and Agriculture Organization (FAO) of the United Nations, meat production is the second or third larg-

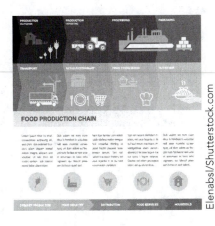

est contributor to environmental problems at every level and at every scale, from global to local. It is implicated in land degradation, air pollution, water shortage, water pollution, species extinction, loss of biodiversity, and climate change. The reports' author Henning Steinfeld stated: "livestock are one of the most significant contributors to today's most serious environmental problems. Urgent action is needed to remedy the situation" (19).

Another writer summarized factory production of meat as follows: "the evidence is strong. It's not simply that meat is a contributor to global warming; it's that it is a huge contributor. Larger, by a significant margin, than the global transportation sector" (20). In other words, if you drive a Prius, and care about the environment, it makes *more* sense to adopt a whole foods mostly plant-based diet, by a significant margin.

Why is this so? One reason is methane. Livestock emit methane gas from both ends of the cow, and in such gigantic amounts that scientists increasingly view methane emissions as one of the most significant threats to the earth's climate (21). The previously mentioned UN FAO report states that livestock production is responsible for 65% of nitrous oxide (another greenhouse gas) produced by human activities. The report concludes that overall, livestock production is responsible for 18% of greenhouse gas emissions, a bigger share than all of the SUVs, cars, trucks, buses, trains, ships, and planes in the world combined.

Scientific American published a report in 2009 with similar warnings. Producing beef for the table has a surprising environmental cost: it releases prodigious amounts of heat trapping greenhouse gases (22). Emissions from producing a pound of beef are 58 times greater than those from producing a pound of potatoes.

There is a tremendous amount of information about the environmental consequences of our current factory food production system and its negative effects to our planet if we don't change our ways. Everywhere I looked when researching this book, I was faced with information that affected me deeply. I wanted to turn away, but couldn't. How could I continue with writing this book in the face of such overwhelming suffering?

4 Step MAC Guide

Mindfully
acknowledge
attention
accept
choose

Fortunately, we have the MAC model. I found that I needed to use the MAC model of mindfulness in order to stay engaged in my research, and ultimately my body.

> The MAC Model: To live mindfully the "Mindful MAC Model" reminds us to practice four simple steps to approach each and every precious moment: (1) acknowledging, (2) paying attention to, (3) accepting without judgment, and (4) making a choice in all of your experiences. Simply stated, it's your life, make each experience count. (18).

If I choose to simply turn away from the pain and suffering I feel, then I choose to move mindlessly through life, ignoring how my food is produced and where it comes from. Instead, if I choose to practice mindfulness skills and sit with the feelings engendered by learning about the food system, I can notice, and have an opportunity to take a different action if I desire to do so. Remember that mindfulness does not prescribe any one type of action; simply we have the opportunity to notice, and pay attention to our thoughts and feelings, and discover with curiosity if our values and interests align with our actions, a process known as right action (23).

Once I was able to settle myself, and notice my own judgment, I was able to resume my work. I was buoyed by opposite, more encouraging facts such as those presented by Environmental Defense, who calculates that if every meat eater in the United States swapped just one meal of chicken per week for a vegetarian meal, the carbon savings would be equivalent to taking half a million cars off the road (24). Now that's something within my control! This new enthusiasm for my own efforts allowed me to begin to rethink my plate.

Jacek Chabraszewski/Shutterstock.com

Alis Photo/Shutterstock.com

RETHINKING YOUR PLATE

Looking at the environmental impacts of big factory farming and the distribution of food can be overwhelming. It can also be limiting, if we turn toward some aspects, and ignore others.

One organization (25) has used a smart and useful way to examine our food system. Called the SEED model, which stands for Social, Economic, Environmental, and Diet/Heath, we can look at the food system through four lenses:

Using the SEED model (26), we notice the intersections of the food system. If we look at just one of the components, we miss the other pieces. The social aspect of the food system is composed of food and traditions, taste and flavor, and any environmental impacts. When we consider the environmental sphere, we notice the issues of climate change, topsoil loss, and farming practices. The economic sphere is comprised of food costs, trade policies, and crop subsidies. And finally, when we consider diet and health, we see diseases, hunger, and food safety.

Doremi/Shutterstock.com

Thinking about what is on our plates brings us both good and bad news.

Good News	Bad News
• Food hubs	• Genetically modified crops
• Farm to school programs	• Pink slime
• Local food	• Obesity & diabetes
• Farmer's markets	• Water
• Sustainable CSA food systems	• Antibiotics
• Plant-based diet can feed 10 billion	• Meat-centric diet can only feed 4 million

The good news is that regional and local food systems are working together to reconnect people to their food. This effort brings healthier food to consumers, with more diversity, and in a sustainable model that is kinder to the environment (26). Consumers benefit from knowing where their meals come from, connecting them to the food, the farmer, and the community. This approach encourages mindful consumption of natural resources and mindful eating of our meals.

On the negative side, the industrial food system results in increases in productivity and decreases in costs to consumers but destroys the livelihood of rural communities. Food production becomes anonymous; people get sick from safety issues caused by mass production, contaminants in the food production system, and overcrowding in CAFOs. Large-scale factory food production is eroding our soil, and polluting our environment. This encourages mindless eating and mindless consumption of natural resources. It is also not sustainable.

As you read this section use your MAC Guide to track your experience. Are you reacting or responding? When we look at food using the SEED model, we find that any individual item of food becomes very complex. Government policies, which increase corporate consolidation, result in a few controlling the entire process from seeds, to plants, to products, to distribution. Just a few corporations control the following inputs: seeds, * Farms, * Processing, * Trucks, * Brands, and * Grocery Stores. This is called vertical integration, which means cheap food (27). Vertical integration results in the following:

- 50% of all groceries are purchased at four supermarket chains
- One in three of all children in the United States are overweight or obese
- Around the world, soil is being eroded at the rate of 36,000 square miles destroyed per year (the size of the State of Indiana)

Mindscanner/Shutterstock.com

- 1,835 miles is the distance the average carrot in the United States travels to reach the dinner table on a truck
- 800,000 farm workers are in the United States, many living far below the poverty line
- 40% of the food grown in the United States is lost due to spoilage.

Looking at the results of our factory farm system of food production, are you convinced that we can do better? I am convinced that we *must* do better—the future depends upon skillful action. What is your next step living in your community and in your personal life?

ALTERNATIVE CHOICES—WHY IT MATTERS

We all have responsibility for creating an alternative food system. We are also responsible for knowing that due to the intersections of the food system, change is complex and interconnected. There are things we all can do as individuals to make more sustainable, mindful choices about the food we eat and our environment.

1. Be curious about where your food comes from.
   a. Eat in season. Having blueberries shipped from South America in the winter is a waste of fossil fuel as well as an unsatisfying taste experience. Choose local produce whenever possible—that way you make sure it is in season.
2. Advocate for labeling transparency.
   a. Want to know where your meat comes from? Do you want to avoid GMOs? Right now, you're on your own since there is no requirement to tell the consumer this information. Get involved in local and national organizations that advocate for transparency in food labeling.
2. Shorten the distance between where food is grown and you.
   a. This sensible piece of advice limits the amount of finite resources needed to bring food to your plate. Looking for a calculator? Try Falls Brook Centre's Online Calculator (28).
4. Eat and cook yourself. Make fresh, whole foods—mostly plants. If you choose to eat meat, chicken, or pork, buy organic, grass fed, sustainably raised animal protein. Eat smaller amounts, as is done in other countries. It's more expensive, so eat less.
5. Ask questions.

The surgeon general has called obesity an epidemic that costs our health care system close to $100 billion a year (29), but we must go much further in educating each other and us about the consequences of poor food choices. The effort deserves the same attention we gave to educating Americans about smoking's ill effects. In that case, we launched widespread public awareness campaigns, issued government warnings, and taxed cigarettes.

It may not make sense to tax junk food, but government and others can encourage better choices. The "Buy Fresh Buy Local" campaign, coordinated by national nonprofit Food Routes (30), marks a good beginning, as do regional efforts like Arizona's Community Food Connections (31).

We have a well-developed system for growing and shipping large volumes of corn and soybeans—grain elevators, warehouses, and railroads—and we must create an equally functional system for local food, which would include warehousing and shipping facilities for local produce and the capacity for processing organic meat. Those systems are being built in Northern California and a few other places, but that's it. Worse yet, within the current crop subsidy system, farmers encounter disincentives if they want to switch from commodity production (corn and soybeans) to fruits or vegetables.

Financially and sustainably, rebuilding local food systems is economically feasible. Consider the tremendous demand for organic food, which has arrived in nearly every corner of the United States. Restaurants and consumers are increasingly demanding fresh, healthy, locally produced food. One organization (32) is working to estimate the demand for organic food. They found in Chicago there is nearly $500 million worth of organic food desired by local consumers, but nearly all of this is being shipped from out of state. The economic benefit of rebuilding local food systems go to those who need it most: small farmers not equipped to producing corn at large, industrial scale; fast-disappearing farmers on the fringe who work close to local markets; and people whose troubled and damaged urban neighborhoods (think inner city Detroit, and parts of New Orleans, as examples) may become warehousing and distribution districts. A study by Michael H. Shuman (32) estimated that shifting 20% of metro Detroit's food spending to food and beverages that are locally grown and processed would increase the region's annual economic output by nearly $3.5 billion, create more than 35,000 "greencollar" jobs, and lead to a nearly $155 million gain in business taxes. Detroit is taking note, and things are changing there, exactly as Shuman suggested in 2007.

It may not be realistic to imagine the end of all-large scale factory type faming. To feed a nation as populated as the United States, some large-scale farming is probably inevitable.

Nevertheless, different organizing principles can guide that production. Companies such as Cascadian Farms, Horizon Organic, and Organic Valley, as three examples, are producing meat, milk, and vegetables in great volume while using organic feed (without antibiotics), organic fertilizer, and natural pesticides (32). Smaller farmers such as Skagit River Ranch (33) have demonstrated that the sustainability of "green" farming practices. They simply cannot produce enough grass fed beef, humanely treated chicken and eggs to feed the demand.

Because large organic farms suffer from some of the same problems as large-scale traditional farms—animals are confined in large numbers and products are often shipped long distances—smaller-scale local food systems should be developed to the fullest extent possible.

What About Green Legislation?

Many advocate for using government to jumpstart the redevelopment of local food systems. In Illinois, for instance, food advocates were disturbed by the fact that less than 1,000 acres of central Illinois farmland is dedicated to fruit and vegetable production—and that's out of 5.4 million acres of fertile farmland in 16 counties. In 2014, a compromise Farm Bill was signed into law by President Obama, with a landmark change that the environmental community fought hard for: Farmers and ranchers are eligible for subsidies only when they conserve their lands, such as wetlands, grasslands, and erodable land. That's critically important because about half the land in the contiguous United States is crop, range, or pasture land. Previous versions of the Farm Bill encouraged destroying these areas to plant more crops. This signals a tremendous change and bodes well for the future of environmentally sustainable farming in the United States (34). Although imperfect, the bill is celebrated by the Organic Trade Association, because there's more funding for the National Organic Program. It will be used to enforce organic standards, improve technology and negotiate international trade agreements, as well as funding research on organic farming practices and providing financial assistance for small farms to afford organic certification.

Robert Kneschke/Shutterstock.com

Also for the first time, organic farmers, distributors, and marketers will have access to the same agriculture research and promotion programs that always have been helpful to conventional farmers.

This is exciting for those such as myself who encourage a more sustainable approach to farming and crop production in this country. I'm also excited by the many nonprofits (30) working to educate consumers or reform the food production and distribution system. You might find it encouraging that the 2007 *New Oxford American Dictionary* word of the year was *locavore*—a person who eats locally grown food. That says a lot about national awareness of the issue. Perhaps, in another 20 years, we will see a vibrant and diverse agricultural landscape—a revitalization of the neighborhood and landscape America has in its history, embedded in our collective consciousness, and much more closely aligned with our fantasy of what the farm means to all of us.

Curious how far your food travels? Use the Food Miles Calculator to find out just how many miles your food needs to journey to reach your plate! It might make a difference and inspire you to choose local!! (35)

Eating locally and in season isn't always possible in the dry Arizona desert where I live. Citrus season, however, is amazing, with organic oranges right off my own tree! I make this marinade for tofu with juice freshly squeezed from my oranges. It is delicious!

Sweet Citrus Marinade

½ cup freshly squeezed orange juice

¼ cup freshly squeezed lemon juice

¼ cup low sodium soy sauce or tamari

2 teaspoons maple syrup

1 tablespoon minced fresh ginger

1 tablespoon olive oil

1 minced jalapeno pepper

2 cloves garlic, minced

Mix all the ingredients together in a shallow dish large enough to use for marinating a small package of extra firm tofu. Marinate the tofu following drying it off with paper towels and pressing it between two plates, and put some weight on it. This presses out all the water it's packed in and allows room for the marinade flavor. Press the tofu for 30 minutes to one hour. Cut the tofu into slices no thicker than ¼ inch. Place the tofu into the marinade and allow it to soak in the refrigerator for up to 8 hours. When ready to bake the tofu, reheat the oven to 450 degrees F, arrange the tofu planks on a baking sheet and bake for 15 minutes, flip, spoon a little marinade on each piece, and bake for 10 more minutes. Flip once more and bake a final 5 minutes. Each piece should be a little burned on the edges. Let it sit for a few minutes, and then cut into whatever size pieces you need for a stir fry or other dish with tofu. Enjoy!

REFERENCES

1. http://www.kyphilom.com/www/seattle.html for Ted Perry's version of Chief Seattle's Thoughts.
2. USDA. 2014. "Family Farming in the United States." *Amber Waves.* [March 14, 2015]. Available from: http://www.ers.usda.gov/amber-waves/2014-march/family-farming-in-the-united-states.aspx#. VQS7VGTF_AZ.
3. Grace. 2013. "How Industrial Food Impacts Your Health." *Sustainable Table.org.* [March 14, 2015]. Available from: http://www.sustainabletable.org/941/how-industrial-food-impacts-your-health.
4. Murphy, S. 2008. "Globalization and Corporate Concentration in the Food and Agriculture Sector." *Development* 51, 527–533. doi: 10.1057/dev.2008.57.
5. Tufts University. "Hogging the Market: How Powerful Meat Packers Are Changing Our Food System and What We Can Do About It." *Leveling the Field—Issue Brief #4.* [March 14, 2015]. Available from: http://www.ase.tufts.edu/gdae/Pubs/rp/AAI_Issue_Brief_4.pdf.
6. Factory Farm Map. 2010. "Factory Farm Nation: How America Turned its Livestock Farms into Factories." *Food and Water Watch.* [March 14, 2015]. Available from: http://www.factoryfarmmap.org/wp-content/uploads/2010/11/FactoryFarmNation-web.pdf.
7. Howard, P. 2013. "Seed Industry Structure." [March 14, 2015]. Available from: https://msu.edu/~howardp/seedindustry.html.
8. Organic Consumers Association. 2013. "US and Monsanto Dominate Global Market for GM Seeds." [March 14, 2015]. Available from: https://www.organicconsumers.org/essays/us-and-monsanto-dominate-global-market-gm-seeds.
9. Shah, A. B. 2010. "Global Issues: Social, Political, Economic and Environmental Issues that Affect Us All." [March 14, 2015]. Available from: http://www.globalissues.org/article/240/beef.
10. Bloomberg Business. 2013. "America Must Stop Exporting Obesity." [March 14, 2015]. Available from: http://www.bloomberg.com/bw/articles/2013-01-06/america-must-stop-exporting-obesity.
11. Centers for Disease Control and Prevention. 2014. "Frequently Asked Questions About Antibiotic Resistance and Food Safety." [March 14, 2015]. *National Antimicrobial Resistance Monitoring System.* Available from: http://www.cdc.gov/narms/faq.html.
12. Pimentel, D. and Pimentel, M. 2003. "Sustainability of Meat-Based and Plant-Based Diets and the Environment." *American Society for Clinical Nutrition* 78 (3), pp. 6605–6635.
13. Campbell, T. C. 2013. *Whole: Rethinking the Science of Nutrition.* Dallas, TX: Benbella Books.
14. Pimentel, D. 1995. "Environmental and Economic Costs of Soil Erosion and Conservation Benefits." *Science* 267 (5201), pp. 1117–1123.
15. Klein, E. 2009. "Gut Check: Here's the Meat of the Problem." [Webpage]. *The Washington Post,* July 29. Available from: http://www.washingtonpost.com/wp-dyn/content/article/2009/07/28/AR2009072800390.html.

16. Robbins, J. 2010. *The Food Revolution: How Your Diet Can Help Save Your Life and Our World*. San Francisco: Conari Press.

17. FAO of the United Nations. 2007. "Livestock's Long Shadow: Environmental Issues and Opinions." In *United Nations, 2006, Rome, Italy*, ed. Hennings Steinfeld, Rome, Italy: Communication Division—FAO.

18. Napoli, M. 2010. *Tools for Mindful Living: Steppingstones for Practice*. 2nd ed. Dubuque, IA: Kendall Hunt. p. 29.

19. Food and Agriculture Organization of the United Nations. 2006. *Deforestation Causes Global Warming*. [Website]. [February 2, 2015]. Available from: http://www.fao.org/newsroom/en/news/2006/1000385/index.html.

20. Klein, E. 2009. "Gut Check: Here's the Meat of the Problem." [Webpage]. *The Washington Post*, July 29. Available from: http://www.washingtonpost.com/wp-dyn/content/article/2009/07/28/AR2009072800390.html.

21. Singh, M. 2014. "Gassy Cows Are Warming the Planet and They're Here to Stay." NPR.org. [March 14, 2015]. Available from: http://www.npr.org/blogs/thesalt/2014/04/11/301794415/gassy-cows-arewarming-the-planet-and-theyre-here-to-stay.

22. Fiala, N. 2009. "How Meat Contributes to Global Warming." [Webpage]. *Scientific American*, February. [February 3, 2015]. Available from: http://www.scientificamerican.com/article/the-greenhouse-hamburger/.

23. Zinn, J. K. 1994. *Wherever You Go, There You Are: Mindfulness Meditation in Every Day Life*. New York, NY: Hyperion.

24. Mayo Clinic. 2014. "Meatless Meals: The Benefits of Eating Less Meat." *Nutrition and Healthy Eating*. [March 14, 2015]. Available from: http://www.mayoclinic.org/healthy-living/nutrition-and-healthy-eating/in-depth/meatless-meals/art-20048193.

25. University of Vermont. 2011. "Seed to Plate: How the University of Vermont is Cultivating Food Systems as an Academic Discipline." *Community Development and Applied Economics*. [March 14, 2015]. Available from: http://www.uvm.edu/~cdac/?Page=news&storyID=12535&category=food.

26. University of Vermont. "What's on Your Plate? Food Systems Initiative." [March 15, 2015]. Available from: http://www.uvm.edu.

27. Kilmer, R. L. "Vertical Integration in Agricultural and Food Marketing." *American Journal of Agricultural Economics* 68 (5), Proceedings Issue (December, 1986), pp. 1155–1160.

28. Falls Brook Centre. 2002. "The Food Miles Calculator." [Webpage]. *Falls Brook Centre CA*. [February 3, 2015]. Available from: http://www.fallsbrookcentre.ca/cgi-bin/calculate.pl.

29. Office of the Surgeon General (US); Office of Disease Prevention and Health Promotion (US); Centers for Disease Control and Prevention (US); National Institutes of Health (US). 2001. *The Surgeon General's Call to Action to Prevent and Decrease Overweight and Obesity*. Rockville (MD): Office of the Surgeon General (US). Section 1: *Overweight and Obesity as Public Health Problems in America*. Available from: http://www.ncbi.nlm.nih.gov/books/NBK44210/.

30. "Food Routes Network." [March 14, 2015]. Available from: http://foodroutes.org/.

31. "Phoenix Public Market." [March 14, 2015]. Available from: http://phxpublicmarket.com/openair/.

32. Stanford University. 2008. "Fast Food And The Family Farm." *Stanford Social Innovation Review*. [June 12, 2015]. Available from: http://www.ssireview.org/articles/entry/fast_food_and_the_family_farm .

33. Vogkovich, E. 2015. "Skagit River Ranch." [Website]. [February 15, 2015]. Available from: http://www.skagitriverranch.com/.

34. Green, B. 2014. "Farm Bill Aims to Grow Green Power, Hemp, and Organics." [Website]. *Green Biz*, February 2. Available from: http://www.greenbiz.com/blog/2014/02/03/farm-bill-boosts-green-power-hemp-and-organics.

35. Falls Brook Centre. "Food Miles Calculator." Available from: http://www.//fallsbrookcentre.ca/cgi-bin/calculate.pl.

Mindful Eating Reflection Journal

1. Acknowledge
Describe your experience; what did you choose to eat?

2. Intentional Attention

Describe what you noticed during your mindful eating practice.

BREATH:
BODY:
EMOTIONS:
THOUGHTS:
SENSES:

3. Accept Without Judgment
Describe judgment; acceptance

4. Choose Your Experience
Intention/willingness; new perspective

5. Mindful Meditation/Mindful Eating Experience (Mindful Practice)
What did you notice about your meditation experience this week?

MINDFUL EATING WEEKLY QUIZ

This is a brief snapshot of your mindful eating skills. It is to help you to identify which skills you may want to change or enhance. Circle the best answer. Don't forget to notice what you already do well. After you complete this quiz, write down a mindful eating goal for the week.

Take this quiz each week of the course.

1. I tend to stop eating when I am full

⬅──────────────────────────────────────➡

| All of the time | Most of the time | Occasionally | Sometimes | Almost Never |

2. I eat when I am hungry rather than when I feel emotional

| All of the time | Most of the time | Occasionally | Sometimes | Almost Never |

3. I try not to "pick" at food

| All of the time | Most of the time | Occasionally | Sometimes | Almost Never |

4. I taste each bite before reaching for the next

| All of the time | Most of the time | Occasionally | Sometimes | Almost Never |

5. When I eat, I think about how nourishing the food is for my body

| All of the time | Most of the time | Occasionally | Sometimes | Almost Never |

6. I am nonjudgmental of myself, my body and when I accidentally overeat

| All of the time | Most of the time | Occasionally | Sometimes | Almost Never |

7. I don't multitask while I eat. When I eat, I just eat and focus on the food in front of me

| All of the time | Most of the time | Occasionally | Sometimes | Almost Never |

8. I don't have to eat everything on my plate, I can leave what I don't want

| All of the time | Most of the time | Occasionally | Sometimes | Almost Never |

9. I tend to eat slowly, chewing each bite

| All of the time | Most of the time | Occasionally | Sometimes | Almost Never |

10. I recognize when I slip into mindless eating (zoned out, popping food into my mouth)

| All of the time | Most of the time | Occasionally | Sometimes | Almost Never |

List your Mindful Eating Goals: (ex: learn to be more present when I eat, slow down, stop when I'm full)

CHAPTER 9

Mindful Eating—A Sustainable Practice for Lifelong Weight Maintenance

> *Acknowledging my eating experience*
> *Paying attention to the tastes, smells, and textures*
> *Accepting each bite with joy*
> *Choosing to chew slowly*
> *My mouth waters with delight*
> *Mindfully enjoying the beauty of nature*
>
> (Napoli)

"One hundred years ago all we ate was local, organic food; grass-fed, real whole food. There were no fast-food restaurants, there was no junk food, there was no frozen food. There was just what your mother or grandmother made. Most meals were eaten at home. In the modern age that tradition, that knowledge, is being lost (1)."

When one thinks about eating an image of sitting down with loved ones enjoying a meal may come to mind. Sharing a meal engages us in emotional, social, verbal, and familial ways. If we stop and reflect a moment, the entire process of eating, beginning with choosing foods, often gathered the same day as they were eaten combined with exercise and socializing while collecting food, preparing the foods, often by small groups of family members, and finally eating the foods surrounded by those who gathered and prepared was a mindful event, present in every aspect. All cultures have various ceremonies, traditions, and foods that are relevant to their health and overall well-being. What we eat, in addition to the environment we eat in, has historically been significant in daily life. Today, we unfortunately have developed a problem with food and eating. We eat alone, in our cars, while working at our desks, isolated, and disconnected from others and from the act of eating. In the search for answers, blame has been laid on the food industry, on the reliance we have for fast food, on sugar, on processed foods, on advertising, and even on the diet business (2–7). One of the most devastating results of our problem eating is obesity. Obesity is a problem in our culture; experts call it an "epidemic" and suggest multiple causes and conditions for its increasing prevalence (8, 9). The gathering of food and preparing it in modern cultures is practically non-existent. This eliminates any exercise associated with gathering food which may be a contributing factor to today's obesity.

In an interesting twist, research has considered the habit-driven nature of eating and concludes that familiar behavioral patterns can lead to overeating and unwanted weight gain. Cohen and Babey describe the automatic or unconscious food choices people make as "heuristic", meaning that they rely on familiar experiences and simple procedures to arrive at "adequate, though often imperfect" solutions (10). Heuristic eating, is learned food behavior that is unregulated by deliberative thought and decision making. We might rely on heuristic cues to determine food intake because it may be less taxing than making conscious choices. The problem is this behavioral habit tends to result in food selections that are not optimal. For example, parents who work late and leave work feeling stressed out may be more likely to pick up burgers and fries for themselves and their children than to cook a healthful meal.

Habitual, non-reflective eating choices are difficult to change. Given the wide availability and relative convenience and affordability of most fast food, such behavior tends to support large portion sizes and unhealthy food choices. Research into heuristic eating behavior suggesting a strong unit bias ("a sense that a single entity . . . is the appropriate amount") in human food choices has led to the gradual expansion of portion sizes in many fast-food restaurants and elsewhere.

Take a mindful MAC moment and think about an eating habit you have developed and use the MAC Model to examine the experience:

The MAC Model: To begin learning how to live mindfully we use the "Mindful MAC Model" with its four simple steps to approach each and every precious moment, (1) acknowledging, (2) paying attention to, (3) accepting without judgment, and (4) making a choice in all of your experiences. Simply stated, it's your life, make each experience count (11).

"Another problem is that I haven't had dinner with my family for a week."

What are you aware of? _____

_____

_____

_____

What choice are you making about this habit?

_____

_____

_____

_____

Why this matters: It is remarkable to notice that our eating behavior is habit driven. This might mean that losing weight, or normalizing our weight for life, is simply a matter of developing new habits. This idea is closely aligned with mindfulness practices, which allow us to notice our thoughts, feelings, and behaviors without judgment.

Instead of looking for who or what to blame for our weight and eating issues, what if we take responsibility for our own eating habits, and begin to think about where we eat, who we eat with, and how we eat? Let's consider an approach to eating which has mindfulness at its core, and curiosity, kindness, and gentleness as its process—*Mindful Eating*.

Using the MAC model as our guide, mindful eating is acknowledging our experience just as it is; paying attention to our experience using our senses, body, and emotions; accepting our experience without judgment and making a choice how we show up for our eating experience. Mindfulness practice offers a way to address difficulties with food, eating, and weight in an approach that offers freedom through gentleness and kindness. Eating mindfully allows noticing ourselves with curiosity, kindness, and compassion. This approach to nourishment offers lifelong weight management and effortless weight loss (12).

We begin by answering the following questions:

- Am I aware of when I am hungry?
- Do I eat when I am hungry?
- Do I know what I am hungry for?

Steve Cukrov/Shutterstock.com

Ariwasabi/Shutterstock.com

- What qualities does the food have?
  - Cool, creamy, crunchy, sweet, salty, or savory?
- Am I really hungry for food, or something else?
- Do I stop eating when I am full or satisfied?

If any of these questions are difficult for you to answer, you're not alone. Our fast-paced lives discourage mindful eating, which requires tuning in, paying attention, and staying centered. Many of us eat while distracted, whether we are watching TV, driving, or working. Often, we eat while talking on our smart phones or when surfing the Internet. In the rush to get things done we shovel food down filling one forkful after another and swallow without tasting (13).

Fullness and satisfaction is subtle, and sometimes quickly moving through meals leads to missing the signals the body sends to the brain. Overeating becomes unconscious; far past "enough"; it happens again becoming an established habit. Struggling with weight, we wonder what we're so hungry for. Experts say that it is not only important what we eat, but, how we eat (12,13). By paying attention and making the choice to eat mindfully, through practice the experience of how to be fully satisfied by food without overeating becomes realized.

Angela Waye/Shutterstock.com

RESEARCH ON THE PROBLEM: DIETING AND BODY DISSATISFACTION

Dieting and the pursuit for thinness is entrenched in Western culture and leads to increasing numbers of approaches that restrict calories, promote unhealthy eating, and require external food "rules" to induce weight loss. In addition, traditional diets that restrict calories or entire food groups have little long-term success. These programs have high dropout rates. Participants rarely maintain weight loss and sometimes gain back even more weight than they lost during the diet intervention (14–17). Evidence suggests frequency of dieting directly leads to weight gain (18–22).

In addition to being an unsuccessful way to lose weight, dieting is a known risk factor for unhealthy weight control behaviors, including the development of binge eating and other eating disorders (7, 19).

Instead of considering another diet, which we know from research is doomed to fail, try eating more mindfully. Developing a mindful eating practice is a way to live sustainably, in harmony with your own body appetites and rhythms, offering the possibility of true nourishment.

Are you paying attention? Mindful eating allows us to become aware of the nurturing and positive opportunities that are available through food selection and preparation. When we eat mindfully, we become present to the entire experience of eating, including planning, shopping, cooking, and eating. We use all of our senses to choose food that is both satisfying and nourishing to the body. Our present moment awareness allows us to move beyond habitual and heuristic ways of eating that are driven from old patterns that often lead to overeating, shame, and guilt. Food becomes nourishment for both the body and soul. The

act of eating can be a spiritual practice, and as we tune in to what is right in front of us we cherish every taste, every bite. Mindful eaters eat without judgment, and acknowledge that there is no right or wrong way to eat. Knowing that we can make a choice to eat bite by bite, we are invited to experience the interconnections of earth and all living beings, which elevates the act of eating and connects us to the environment, our communities, our families, and ourselves.

Experiential Exercise in Mindful Eating: Let's Try Our Own Mindful Eating Experience. . . .

4 Step MAC Guide

Mindfully
acknowledge
attention
accept
choose

Let's do an exercise to explore the experience of mindful eating using the MAC Guide. You can read this script into your smart phone, and then play your own voice guiding yourself. Imagine using all of your senses by following the prompts that begin each section of the practice.

Create the space

Choose a place where you can focus on your eating experience without interruption.

Choose the food

Decide upon a food.

Acknowledge your eating experience

Regardless of how the food tastes, smells, or sensations that arise acknowledge them just as they are right now.

Pay attention to your eating experience

Notice all the aspects of your experience that are engaged during your eating . . . thoughts, emotions, body sensations as the food enters your mouth, chewing, swallowing, tastes.

Accept your eating experience without judgment

Embrace the entire mindful eating experience.

Make a choice

Decide how this experience stands out for you and what you can do to bring mindful eating into your daily life.

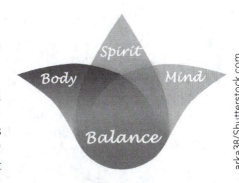

Activity: What was this exercise like? Take a few moments and journal about your experiences. Did you notice anything different? Were you surprised by your experience? How if anything was this experience today different from your usual eating experience? Reflect, and measure your level of hunger and satisfaction. What do you notice? Any surprises? Being curious and gentle with your experience can be a helpful support for this activity.

Mindfully Eating—My Reflections

Is It OK to be Hungry?

Another complication of modern life is our general lack of comfort in our culture with the collection of sensations we call hunger or thirst. We keep a drink always by our side. We often snack all day long. We may say, "I'm not really that hungry" then proceed to devour our food. We make sure we are not hungry later by eating now when we're not all that hungry. Think about the intenseness of the energy behind this "constant filling behavior". Contemplate this one question:

Am I willing to be empty? (23)

As you can see from this question, it is bigger than just about food. Thinking about emptiness and fullness we may actually be considering our whole lives. Sensations of emptiness usually drive us to do something about them, *Now*! Consider another question—What are we afraid of? Are we fearful that we won't find our next meal? Are we afraid to feel the sensations of hunger?

Is it OK for you to feel empty? Many of us would answer "NO". We like the feeling of fullness in our stomachs. It feels comfortable; it is comforting. As we investigate mindful eating, we may find that when we feel empty, beneath the possibility of emptiness, fear arises. We may find that we eat and drink

all day to avoid that feeling. There may be other feelings underneath, as well, including loneliness, boredom, sadness, or isolation. We become trapped as we sit captive by the desire for the mouth and stomach to feel full.

For others, they might answer, Yes, I like feeling empty. For those people, the feeling of emptiness is pleasant and pleasurable. The feeling of fullness may be not pleasant. After eating those who prefer empty may vomit, purge, or over exercise to empty the body of the feeling of fullness. They become trapped, rejecting with harshness the feeling of being full.

Other people would answer: I don't know. They are unaware of whether their stomach or body is signaling hunger. They eat by the clock or they eat when and how much others around them eat. They are trapped; paralyzed by not knowing.

So what is this experience we call Mindful Eating? Mindful eating encourages awareness through the entire experience of eating, including selecting and preparing food. When eating mindfully, food is chosen that is both pleasing and nourishing to the body. Using all of the senses to taste, savor, and enjoy food, eating is pleasurable. This process of deliberately paying attention without judgment allows freedom from reactive, habitual patterns of thinking, feeling, and acting, which often include harsh and unkind statements toward ourselves.

> Mindfulness is "deliberately paying attention, being fully aware of what is happening both inside and outside yourself—in your body, heart and mind—and outside yourself, in your environment. **Mindfulness is awareness without criticism or judgment.**
> [Emphasis added]
> The last sentence is very important. In mindful eating we are not comparing ourselves to anyone else. We are not judging ourselves or others. We are simply witnessing the many sensations and thoughts that come up as we eat. The recipe for mindful eating calls for the warming effect of kindness and the spice of curiosity" (23).

Mindful eating is about making peace with food, and eating according to body needs. When we eat mindfully, we eat to support the body's naturally healthy state, inviting balance, choice, wisdom, and acceptance. Being in the moment and paying attention while we eat allows us to slow down, chew well, taste thoroughly, and enjoy eating. Different than a "diet", mindful eating does not rely on weighting or measuring food, restricting or avoiding certain foods, labeling some foods "good" and others "bad", or counting fat grams or calories. Eating mindfully and encouraging self-acceptance allows us to be free from worrying about body size or "ideal" body weight. Instead, the practice of Mindful Eating encourages the following principles (24):

- **Eat when hungry**. Watch for the body's hunger cues as a signal that it is time to eat. Eat enough to feel satisfied and comfortably full, not stuffed. For most of us, practicing mindful eating means having several small meals throughout the day and one or two planned snacks. Whole foods, mostly plant-based meals including fresh fruits, vegetables, legumes, whole grains, and lean protein, promotes satiety and mealtime satisfaction.
- **Eat in a distraction free zone.** Pay attention to how food tastes, and what feelings arise while eating. Take five or six slow deep breaths when sitting down to eat. Many people benefit from saying silent grace or what

mindful practitioners call a food blessing before beginning meals. No matter which approach is chosen, taking the time to slow down and savor food begins the practice of Mindfulness where the possibility of change begins.

- **Eat what is desired.** Overeating out of deprivation often happens when eating what "should" be eaten instead of what is desired. Labeling certain foods "bad" and restricting food may also lead to searching for food whether hungry or not. Eat rich, satisfying foods in smaller amounts, savoring every bite.

- **Eat until satisfied, not uncomfortable.** It takes about 20 minutes for the brain to register fullness while eating. Slow down, pay attention, and stop before feeling stuffed. Practice putting down the fork in between bites, and take a breath or two to keep relaxed and aware while eating. Wait a bit, and if still hungry, have more. Consistently eating until stuffed means not listening to the bodies' signal of fullness. Occasionally overeating is normal. To change habitual overeating, paying attention allows the possibility of change. Noticing patterns provides the opportunity to choose a different outcome.

- **Use the healthy eating plate model as a guide.** This tool helps develop trust for cues of satisfaction and fullness. Using the Healthy Plate provides freedom from weighting, measuring, or counting calories. Fill ½ the plate with vegetables, ¼ with lean protein, and ¼ with whole grains such as rice, potatoes, pasta, or fresh fruit. This eating approach helps reduce anxiety of how much food is enough or too much. Building mealtime servings with delicious foods in appropriate portions allows healthful eating in exactly the right amounts and the right choices.

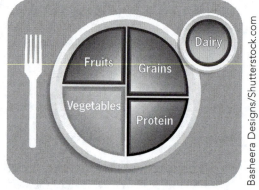

Remember that food is pleasure and should be enjoyed. Using sight, smell, and taste while eating allows all of the senses to participate in the enjoyment of a delicious and nourishing meal. This mindful approach incorporating sensory stimuli encourages eating satisfaction and effortless weight management. Be patient—remember it is called a "practice"—not "perfection"—since it takes time and attention to create a different outcome. The body moves to the weight it is supposed to be, supported through the practice of mindfulness (24).

It's been said that self-observation without judgment is the highest practice of mindfulness (25). It's a challenging task in mindfulness practice, and it can be even more challenging at the dinner table. Each of us has habitual patterns that relate to food and what we eat. Allowing yourself to begin to observe your patterns, and to become mindful and truly focus on the food you eat can feel uncomfortable at first. It can feel unfamiliar to remove the "shoulds" and the guilt. Practicing mindful eating is a sustainable way to improve the experience of eating, and move away from endless dieting and punishing regimens that promote suffering.

It can be challenging to eat mindfully when we experience strong desire for a certain food. Chocolate falls into this category! Here's a recipe that's designed to please your palate and nourish your body. Savor every bite of its delicious goodness. Made with heart healthy avocados, the texture is amazing and creamy. Avocados are a great source of lutein, a type of antioxidant called a carotenoid which works to protect against eye disease. They also contain other carotenoids zeaxanthin, alpha-carotene, and beta-carotene, as well as tocopherol (vitamin E).

Avocados aren't just a rich source of carotenoids by themselves—**they also help you get more of these nutrients from other foods**. Carotenoids are lipophilic (soluble in fat, not water), so eating carotenoid-packed foods such as fruits and vegetables along with monounsaturated-fat-rich avocados helps your body absorb the carotenoids. An easy way to do this by enjoying this delicious dessert at the end of a meal that features vegetables.

Non-Dairy Chocolate Mousse

½ cup pitted dates, pre-soaked in warm water for 15 minutes

½ cup Brown Rice Syrup (or Maple Syrup)

1 teaspoon vanilla extract

1 ½ cup mashed avocados (3 avocados)

¾ cup unsweetened cocoa powder

¼–½ cup water (to thin the mixture, as needed)

Place the soaked and pitted dates, maple syrup, and vanilla in a blender or food processor and process until smooth. Add the avocado and cocoa powder and process until creamy. Stop and scrape down the sides of the blender with a rubber spatula. Add the water and process briefly. Store in a sealed container. You can keep for 3 days in the refrigerator or for 2 weeks frozen. Serve chilled or at room temperature.

Preparation time: 20 minutes

Yield: 4 servings

REFERENCES

1. Hyman, M. 2011. "Eating at home can save your life." [Webpage]. *Huffington Post*. Available from: http://www.huffingtonpost.com/dr-mark-hyman/family-dinner-how_b_806114.html.
2. Mustain, P. (2013). "Dear American consumers: Please don't start eating healthfully. sincerely, the food industry." *Scientific American*. Available from: http://blogs.scientificamerican.com/guest-blog/2013/05/19/dear-american-consumers-please-dont-start-eating-healthfully-sincerely-the-food-industry/.
3. Schlosser, E. (2002). *Fast Food Nation*. London: Penguin Books.
4. Bray, G. A., & Popkin, B. M. (2014). Dietary sugar and body weight: Have we reached a crisis in the epidemic of obesity and diabetes? Health be damned! Pour on the sugar. *Diabetes Care*, 37 (4), pp. 950–956.
5. Mercola, Dr. (2013). How do babies become too fat to toddle? *Mercola.com*, September 23. Available from: http://articles.mercola.com/sites/articles/archive/2013/09/28/childhood-obesity-rates.aspx.
6. Daily Mail Reporter. (2012). Is Advertising To Blame For The Obesity Epidemic?. Available from: http://www.dailymail.co.uk/health/article-2165029/Is-advertising-blame-obesity-epidemic-The-sight-fatty-foods-triggers-hunger-claims-study.html.
7. Pietilainen, K. H., Saarni, S. E., Kaprio, J., & Rissanen, A. (2001). Does dieting make you fat? A twin study. *International Journal of Obesity*, pp. 356–64.
8. Budd, G. M. (2014). The obesity epidemic: Understanding the origins. *The American Journal of Nursing*, 114 (12), pp. 40–46.
9. Peretti, J. (2013). Fat profits: How the food industry cashed in on obesity. *The Guardian*. Available from http://www.theguardian.com/lifeandstyle/2013/aug/07/fat-profits-food-industry-obesity.
10. Cohen, D. A., & Babey, S. H. (2012). Contextual influences on eating behaviors: Heuristic processing and dietary choices. *Obesity Reviews : An Official Journal of the International Association for the Study of Obesity*, 13 (9), 766–779. doi:10.1111/j.1467-789X.2012.01001.x.
11. Napoli, M. (2011). *Tools for mindful living, steppingstones for practice*. Dubuque, IA: Kendall Hunt.
12. Schmidt, L. R. (2014). Mindful eating the ultimate diet. [blog talk radio] *Mindful Benefits*. Available from: http://www.blogtalkradio.com/eatgreatlivewell/2014/09/18/1417-mindful-eating-the-ultimate-diet.
13. Bays, J. C. (2009). *Mindful eating: A guide to rediscovering a healthy and joyful relationship with food*. Boston, MA: Shambhala Publications.
14. Cachelin, F. M., & Regan, P. C. (2006). Prevalence and correlates of chronic dieting in a multi-ethnic U.S. community sample. *Eat and Weight Disorders*, 11 (2), pp. 91–99.

15. Goodrick, G. K., & Foreyt, J. P. (1991). Why treatments for obesity don't last. *Journal of the American Dietetic Association*, 91 (10), pp. 1243–1247.

16. Katan, M. B. (2009). Weight-loss diets for the prevention and treatment of obesity. *New England Journal of Medicine*, 360 (9), pp. 923–925.

17. Mann, T., Tomiyama, A. J., Westling, E., Lew, A. M., Samuels, B., & Chatman, J. (2007). Medicare's search for effective obesity treatments: Diets are not the answer. *American Psychologist*, 62 (3), pp. 220-–233.

18. Dallman, M. F. (2010). Stress-induced obesity and the emotional nervous system. *Trends in Endocrinology Metabolism*, 21 (3), pp. 159–165.

19. Neumark-Sztainer, D., Wall, M., Guo, J., Story, M., Haines, J., & Eisenberg, M. (2006). Obesity, disordered eating, and eating disorders in a longitudinal study of adolescents: How do dieters fare 5 years later? *Journal of the American Dietetic Association*, 106 (4), p. 559–568.

20. Sacks, F. M., Bray, G. A., Carey, V. J. et. al. (2009). Comparison of weight-loss diets with different compositions of fats, proteins, and carbohydrates. *New England Journal of Medicine*, 360 (9), pp. 859–873.

21. Wadden, T. A. (1993). Treatment of obesity by moderate and severe caloric restirction. Results of clinical research trials. *Annals of Internal Medicine*, 119 (7 pt 2), pp. 688–693.

22. Wadden, T. A., Sternberg, J. A., Letizia, K. J., Stunkard, A. J., & Foster, G. D. (1989). Treatment of obesity by very low calorie diet, behavior therapy, and their combination: A five-year perspective. *International Journal of Obesity* 13 (Suppl 2), pp. 39–46.

23. Bays, J. C. (2009). Mindful eating. *Psychology Today*. Available from: http://www.psychologytoday.com/blog/mindful-eating/200902/mindful-eating.

24. The Center for Mindful Eating. (2006). The Principles Of Mindful Eating. *Food for Thought*. Available from http://www.thecenterformindfuleating.org.

25. Wilson, A., (2013). Mindfulness meditation and the brain. *Huffington Post*. Available from: http://www.huffingtonpost.com/kripalu/mindfulness-meditation_b_3238677.html.

MINDFUL EATING REFLECTION JOURNAL

1. Acknowledge
Describe your experience; what did you choose to eat?

2. Intentional Attention

Describe what you noticed during your mindful eating practice.

BREATH:	
BODY:	
EMOTIONS:	
THOUGHTS:	
SENSES:	

3. Accept Without Judgment
Describe judgment; acceptance

4. Choose Your Experience
Intention/willingness; new perspective

5. Mindful Meditation/Mindful Eating Experience (Mindful Practice)
What did you notice about your meditation experience this week?

MINDFUL EATING WEEKLY QUIZ

This is a brief snapshot of your mindful eating skills. It is to help you to identify which skills you may want to change or enhance. Circle the best answer. Don't forget to notice what you already do well. After you complete this quiz, write down a mindful eating goal for the week.

Take this quiz each week of the course.

1. I tend to stop eating when I am full	
All of the time Most of the time Occasionally Sometimes Almost Never	

1. I tend to stop eating when I am full

All of the time   Most of the time   Occasionally   Sometimes   Almost Never

2. I eat when I am hungry rather than when I feel emotional

All of the time   Most of the time   Occasionally   Sometimes   Almost Never

3. I try not to "pick" at food

All of the time   Most of the time   Occasionally   Sometimes   Almost Never

4. I taste each bite before reaching for the next

All of the time   Most of the time   Occasionally   Sometimes   Almost Never

5. When I eat, I think about how nourishing the food is for my body

All of the time   Most of the time   Occasionally   Sometimes   Almost Never

6. I am nonjudgmental of myself, my body and when I accidentally overeat

All of the time   Most of the time   Occasionally   Sometimes   Almost Never

7. I don't multitask while I eat. When I eat, I just eat and focus on the food in front of me

All of the time   Most of the time   Occasionally   Sometimes   Almost Never

8. I don't have to eat everything on my plate, I can leave what I don't want

All of the time   Most of the time   Occasionally   Sometimes   Almost Never

9. I tend to eat slowly, chewing each bite

All of the time   Most of the time   Occasionally   Sometimes   Almost Never

10. I recognize when I slip into mindless eating (zoned out, popping food into my mouth)

All of the time   Most of the time   Occasionally   Sometimes   Almost Never

List your Mindful Eating Goals: (ex: learn to be more present when I eat, slow down, stop when I'm full)

CHAPTER 10

Sustainable Living & Mindful Eating Through the Lifespan

Courtesy of Maria Napoli

> *Simply Green Tea*
> *Each sip cools my palette*
> *Liquid swirls around my mouth*
> *Tastes are awakened*
> *Sweet and tart*
> *Antioxidants nourish*
> *Mindfully satisfied*
>
> (Napoli)

EpicStockMedia/Shutterstock.com

Mindfulness is paying attention to the present moment without judgment. When we are eating mindfully, we use the medicine of mindfulness to cure the disease of desire. Paying attention in the moment allows our focused awareness to slow us down in ways that provide us the opportunity to deeply look at our habits. Moments of mindfulness can help us break free from our automatic responses to mindlessly eat. When we mindfully decide to eat cookies, cake, or other "forbidden" foods, we begin to cultivate the wise concept of choice. This takes us off of automatic pilot, offering us a glimpse of freedom, hope, and opportunity.

Arriving at the last chapter of *Sustainable Living & Mindful Eating*, you are coming to a new beginning! In this book, you have been invited to reflect upon your own life and relationship to food and eating and contemplate choices or changes. You have been reminded of the power of mindfulness practices, creating space for reflection and *feeling*. You may have noticed how the many habits of food and eating are adopted unconsciously with impact to us, our communities, and even our planet. With a more mindful approach, you may realize that being a certain weight or eating only certain kinds of foods may no longer be as important. You may now notice that learning more about food, its power for nourishment, and connecting us to all living beings through mindfulness may be more important than achieving a certain weight or body shape. If this is true for you, the journey of mindful eating poses wonderful opportunities for self-inquiry, self-improvement, and possibly improved health. Rather than focus on a destination, you may find the journey to be the more interesting path.

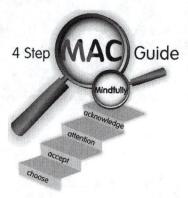

Mindful Eating Is

- The ability to look deeply at the food we eat. We see that it contains the earth, the air, the rain, the sun, and the effort of farmers and all of those who process, transport, and sell us the food. Eating with full awareness allows us mindfulness of all of the right effort required to provide our meals. This awareness can nurture our appreciation of the support we get from others and from nature.

It may be exciting to contemplate a future of living mindfully, eating in tune with your body rhythms, your desires, and all of the natural world. A suggestion for your journey is to begin living and eating mindfully *now*, right this moment. This moment is all we have, so let's begin.

Take a Mindful Moment

Sit in an upright and dignified way, with your hands resting on your legs, palms open to the ceiling. Observe your breathing. Without changing or manipulating your breath just notice its natural rhythm. Breathing in, breathing out; noticing the pattern of the breath like waves on the ocean. As you breathe in, feel the belly expand; as you breathe out, notice its contraction. Easy breath in, and out.

Let's begin our meditation by practicing the ocean breath.

1. Place your open palm close to your mouth. Breathe in and exhale through your mouth. Notice the breath on your hand. (Remember making window fog as a child with your breath).
2. Next—take a breath—inhale, then exhale with mouth closed—pushing the breath toward the back of your throat. (Notice the ocean sound on the exhale).

   You may notice softening in your body. If not, that's OK; resist the temptation to judge or analyze the experience of breathing. Bring your attention to the thought of your favorite food. Try not to judge any choice; simply notice what happens in your body. As you breathe in and out, riding the waves of your breath, just watch what happens to your body as you think about your beloved food. Follow this for six complete breath cycles; then, gently, open your eyes and come back into the room.

What did you notice? Take a few moments and journal some thoughts that came to mind as you sat with your breath and thought about your favorite food. Breathe—reflect—notice—consider.

Cristian Amoretti/Shutterstock.com

_____

_____

_____

_____

_____

YOUR PASSPORT TO SUSTAINABLE LIVING & MINDFUL EATING

In the spirit of a sustainable way to approach mindful eating throughout your life, I offer to you my 10 "travel tips" for the lifetime journey of mindful eating. These suggestions to promote healthful living and a more mindful presence are my form of an offering to you, the reader.

Mj007/Shutterstock.com

Sustainable living, mindful eating suggestion #1: **Food as Energy: Know Yourself.**

When we eat foods appropriate to our own *individual needs* we extract energy from the environment in harmony with the natural world. Learning how to honor and respect your own body rhythms, you can become more skillful in eating what your body needs in the right amounts. Resist the temptation to run toward any one "diet" or approach to eating. Instead, contemplate the energetic nature of food itself, and understand how transforming this stored energy source can nourish you in ways that may seem unimaginable.

Quick Tip: Begin a regular mindfulness practice. Research with compulsive overeaters suggests that mindfulness-based approaches reduce overeating, improve emotional and behavioral dysregulation, and promote internalization of change (1).

Sustainable living, mindful eating suggestion #2: **Food as Fuel.**

**Food as Fuel
Checklist**

Food	Yes	No
Satisfied with quality	x	
Looks like food?	x	
Cannot pronounce		x

Use this checklist next time you go out to eat or when thinking about eating. You'll find this helpful in noticing if your food meets your body's requirements for supporting its growth and development.

The body's ability to adapt in the face of always changing conditions is crucial, and only possible because of its own innate ability to self-regulate. Begin to pay attention to the food you are eating. Are you satisfied with the quality? Does it look like food? It may not be something recognizable, in a package with ingredients that you can't pronounce or understand. Remember that through eating we transform plants and animals into mitochondria, our "cellular power plants" that generate the chemical energy we need to fuel all of our life's functions (2). Is your fuel premium grade, regular, or unleaded? Pay attention to the needs of your own mitochondria and remember their job is immense: cell differentiation, cell death and turnover, cell growth: repair, replacement, and change. Supporting growth, repair, and replacement is an inside job, and your obligation is to provide nourishment needed to support your body's own innate self-regulation.

Quick Tip: Read labels. Reading the nutrition facts label and utilizing the information it contains can help you improve your eating habits. College students who use the nutrition facts label tend to consume fewer calories; less cholesterol, total fat, saturated fat, sodium and sugar; and more fiber than people who don't make use of these labels, according to a study published in the *Journal of the American Dietetic Association* in August 2010 (3). Once you are familiar with the information contained on food labels, it is easy to use them to change your diet for the better.

Sustainable living, mindful eating suggestion #3: **Understand how certain foods affect your emotions. Notice how certain emotions affect your eating patterns.**

From an early age, we learn that avoiding pain is associated with a food reward. As infants, we cry from hunger and we are calmed by Mother's milk. Our earliest associations before conscious awareness include the urge for nourishment, involving pain, and suffering mitigated by sweet liquid goodness. This primal connection is necessary for life itself—we must have food to survive.

With conscious awareness, we can begin to notice just how quickly, often, and without thinking we feed ourselves in response to *any type* of pain. Hunger pains are habitually addressed by feeding, even when we are not physically hungry.

> **Quick Tip:** Slow down your eating or drinking. The hungrier we are, the more important it is to eat slowly with attention. Slowing down allows us to notice if we *even are hungry*. Since much of eating is habit driven, and often a response to strong emotions, slowing down provides the opportunity to notice what is happening in our bodies. This may help us see if it is beyond hunger. Stress is shown to be a cause of unwanted eating (4), so taking three slow, deep breaths before eating can help right the stress reflex.

<u>Sustainable living, mindful eating suggestion #4</u>: **<u>Know the difference between real foods, fake foods, and junk foods. Choose skillfully.</u>**

Food-like substances are processed foods made from real food that has been put through chemical processes and are filled with chemicals and preservatives. Junk foods have very little food in them. Instead, they are made of highly processed foods, hydrogenated fats, chemicals and preservatives, and anything made with "refined white flour". Fake foods are made primarily of chemicals, and usually contain gums and sugar as fillers (5). Knowing more about real, whole foods and choosing them more often is a ticket to a lifetime of sustainable and mindful eating.

> **Quick Tip:** Avoid eating fast food. Research shows that eating fast food among children in the United States seems to have a negative effect on dietary quality in ways that increase risk for obesity (6).

<u>Sustainable living, mindful eating suggestion #5</u>: **<u>Find ways to balance food and pleasure.</u>**

Sustainable living and mindful eating for life involves pleasurable eating, too. Remember that it is not necessary to eliminate *all* of the less desirable food choices we make. We all enjoy the occasional cheeseburger, fries, Coke, or potato chips. When we begin to understand the consequences of changing an occasional treat into an everyday event, we can make skillful choices about how many of these "treats" we are willing to eat.

> **Quick Tip:** Find ways to work special foods into your diet. Remember that treats are designed for occasional indulgences; keep a food diary or journal to track the percentages of "healthy" versus less healthful food choices. Notice your own patterns with food and eating, and find ways to have a treat, or an indulgence, once or twice a week. Studies show that people who keep track of what they eat lose weight faster than those who don't. The researchers noted that the more detailed and consistent the food journaling, the better results you're likely see (7).

<u>Sustainable living, mindful eating suggestion #6</u>: **<u>Limit your added sugar intake.</u>**

Sugar added to foods really does appear to be a big problem (8). Foods with a lot of added sugar contribute extra calories to your diet but provide little nutritional value. In addition, added sugar is often found in foods that also contain solid fats. It is in *all* packaged foods. Over 80% of the food sold in the supermarket contains added sugar.

   Eating too many foods with added sugar and solid fats sets the stage for potential health problems, such as poor nutrition, weight gain, increased triglycerides, and tooth decay. Most experts now recommend no more than 100 calories a day from added sugar (for women) or 150 per day (for men). That's about six teaspoons for women and nine for men.

Most Americans get more than 22 teaspoons (or 355 calories) of added sugar a day. This can easily add up to a weight gain of 3–4 pounds a month if we're not careful. Choose natural sources of sweet food instead, like fresh fruit, to help with cravings for sweet foods.

Quick Tip: Can the cola. Drinking calories is a one-way ticket to added weight gain. Don't be confused: anytime we drink calories (especially alcohol, which has 2½ times the calories per gram as carbohydrates or protein calories), our body is not able to "register" our intake in the same way as if we chew whole foods. Added or concentrated forms of sugar are in soda, energy drinks, sports drinks, smoothies, coffee drinks, juices, and alcohol—causing unwanted weight gain. Sugar calories are empty calories—they just add pounds (9).

Don't worry about the "sugar" that is in fruit. Whole fresh fruit, or fruit that you use in a smoothie that you make yourself, doesn't appear to be a problem. The fiber that is also in fresh whole foods such as fruits and vegetables acts as a "buffer" to natural sugars in foods, slowing down our digestive process which helps keep our blood sugar stable. If you pair some fresh fruit with a healthy form of fat or protein (apple and nut butter, orange and nonfat yogurt, carrots and hummus) you benefit from this winning combination. For more "healthy pairings" go to The Mindful Nutritionists' YouTube page (10).

Sustainable living, mindful eating suggestion #7: **Give your food a face.**

Mindfulness requires of us that we wake up to what is. Rather than judging whether certain foods are good or bad, we simply notice other things—how food makes us feel when we eat it; how we respond to cravings, desire and strong drives for certain foods; whether or not what we eat aligns with our beliefs and values. This means that eating mindfully is facilitated by learning more about food—where it comes from, how it is grown, who harvests it, how does it get to us (truck, train, plane), and how we prepare it. Since food is energy that nourishes us, converting vitalism from plants and animals to our own use, give your food a face. If your food comes from an animal source, how was that animal treated? Was it factory farmed, or humanely raised and butchered? If it is a plant, were chemicals used, or was it grown organically?

Honor yourself and the food that nourishes you by giving it a face. This doesn't mean that plants are good and animals are bad—just take time to learn more about how your food gets to your plate. Sustainable living and mindful eating asks this from all of us.

Quick Tip: What about GMOs? The issue is complex. Food that is genetically modified has the potential to contribute to allergies, as well as antibiotic resistance (11). The facts are that there have been no human studies to see if eating GMO foods causes any problems for humans (12). For now, many experts recommend avoiding genetically modified foods and advocating for transparent labeling. With mindfulness, once you notice you have the choice to change (or not). Unless foods are labeled as to how they are modified, you as the consumer have no choice.

Non-GMO foods are voluntarily labeled, and more widely available than ever. Choose non-GMO foods until safety studies can demonstrate little or no risk to humans from consuming them.

Sustainable living, mindful eating suggestion #8: **Choose to eat a wide variety of whole, fresh foods, mostly plants.**

In the *Permanente Journal* last year, the official peer-reviewed publication of our nation's largest managed care organization, a "Nutrition Update for Physicians" was published, which concluded that "Healthy eating maybe best achieved with a plant-based diet," which they defined as a diet that encourages whole plant-based foods and discourages meat, dairy products, and eggs as well as empty calorie junk. To quote their conclusion: "Research shows that plant-based diets are cost-effective, low-risk interventions that may lower body mass index, blood pressure, HbA1C, and cholesterol levels. They may also reduce the number of medications needed to treat chronic diseases and lower ischemic heart disease mortality rates. Physicians should consider recommending a plant-based diet to all their patients, especially those with high blood pressure, diabetes, cardiovascular disease, or obesity" (13).

The Dietary Guidelines Advisory Committee is a governmental committee responsible for updating the Dietary Guidelines for Americans. This position paper becomes the starting point for federal recommendations and policy regarding nutrition standards for healthy Americans. In their 2015 preliminary position statement, they are suggesting all Americans adopt a whole foods, mostly plant-based diet for health and sustainability reasons (14). There is a ways to go before final recommendations are issued, but it is likely that moving to a more plant-based diet will be a cornerstone of the recommendations since that position aligns with what most nutrition and scientific experts on health and longevity have been saying for many years.

> **Quick Tip:** Eat real foods. Mostly plants. Not too much (15). This wisdom from Michael Pollan is a sensible strategy for a sustainable, mindful eating mode. Avoiding issues with processed foods, added sugars, salt, and other nonfood items, real foods help nourish our bodies the way nature intended. Eating real foods allows you to meet all of your nutritional needs in an effortless, delicious way. Learn about real foods; take a cooking class, read cookbooks. Your health is worth it!

Sustainable living, mindful eating suggestion #9: **Eat mindfully in the right amount.**

Mindfulness practices encourage us to view things with "right" mind. Ancient wisdom encourages us to follow the eight-fold path, which uses the adjective "right": right view, right mindfulness, right effort, and so on. In this way, right means appropriate, beneficial, leading to happiness and freedom. What then is the "right" amount of food?

Eating the right amount is consistent with the concept of "just enough". This is not a fixed amount. It changes according to circumstances. One thing is for certain—we can find just enough using our mindfulness practice. By paying attention to how we feel before, during, and after our meals, we can learn for ourselves what "just enough" is. In so doing, we encourage learning how to find the right amount of food for ourselves.

In the words of teacher Ajahn Chah, we learn about right amount:

> "When you think that after another five mouthfuls you'll be full, stop and drink some water and you will have eaten just the right amount. If you sit or walk afterward you won't feel heavy . . . But that's not the way we usually do it. When we feel full we take another five mouthfuls. That's what the mind tells us. It doesn't know how to teach itself ... Someone who lacks a genuine wish to train their mind will be unable to do it. Keep watching your mind" (16).

> **Quick Tip:** Breathe before eating. As you sit down to eat, stop, pause and take five breaths. Then begin. Halfway through your meal, stop, pause, and take five more breaths. Notice your level of fullness and hunger. Thinking about fullness from a scale of 1 (famished) to 10 (stuffed and uncomfortable) gauge your level of hunger. Ideally, we stop eating at 6 or 7—and never wait to eat below 3.

Sustainable living, mindful eating suggestion #10: **Practice gratitude.**

Food is abundant in our culture. So is disharmony with food and eating. Americans are plagued with unbalanced and negative relationships with food and eating. Access to more information about food and health only makes matters worse. Should I eat carbs? No Carbs? Paleo? Vegan? Vegetarian? Avoid gluten? Avoid sugar? The list goes on and on. This distress about food and eating is due to our affluence and ready access to food. When we have too much, something happens to our sense of gratitude. When we lose touch with feeling grateful, we become more and more unhappy with our lives. Taking our bodies and our health for granted, we ignore how we feel, moving only toward pleasure.

Taking food for granted, without gratitude, we ignore what is on our plate. We stop paying attention, smelling, and tasting. That's why it's so easy for us to eat "fake" food; protein powders with no flavor, bars that taste like cardboard, "dead" food fried beyond recognition.

Finding our way back to simple gratitude for the magic of food and nourishment is the way home. Through mindfulness, we can look more deeply into the act of eating, rediscovering the wonder and amazement of our abundant choices. Mindful eating allows us to really look at our food; appreciating the colors, shapes, sizes, play of light and shadows, and taste of the first bite.

> "In this food I clearly see the presence of the entire universe supporting my existence" (17).

When we look deeply into our food, our hearts reach out to the many forms of life that are sacrificed every day to provide our abundance. We repay this sacrifice by being alive to them and the food we choose to eat, which has been provided for our needs. We send loving kindness to all of those who have benefitted us, including the plants and animals, and all the people who have helped to bring the bounty to our table. We look deeply, with gratitude arising without effort.

> **Quick Tip:** Before meals, acknowledge your food with gratitude. Here is one example: "May I receive this food as a gift from the earth, the sky, and all the living beings and their hard work that made it possible for me to nourish this body and mind."

We eat and drink at the opportunity to enter a special place of noticing, paying attention to our body and breath, and our emotions. Every time we pick up our fork, we can notice the weight of our silverware, feel our body, connect to the breath, and find happiness and peace. As we find happiness in the most basic activities of our lives, including breathing, walking, eating, drinking, and lying down to sleep, we can glimpse the possibility of how to become happy and at ease in our lives. My wish for you is to find your way home to your birthright—a place of peace, happiness, nourishment, and calm. It is right at the end of your fingertips, on top of your plate, inside your drinking cup. May you and all beings be happy. May you and all beings be healthy. May you and all beings always have enough to eat. May you and all beings be at peace.

Here is a sweet finish for the end of your journey. Enjoy this nourishing recipe using bananas and gluten free flours. You may find that you enjoy this version of a traditional favorite more than you imagined!

GLUTEN FREE BANANA BREAD

Ingredients: 1 cup brown rice flour1 cup white rice flour 1/4 cup each potato starch flour and tapioca flour1 teaspoon xanthan gum1 tablespoon gluten free baking powder 1/2 teaspoon salt 1 tablespoon *egg replacer such as Ener-G (dry ingredients mixed) 1/2 cup butter (or canola oil) 2/3 cups honey, maple syrup or brown sugar 1-1/2 cups thoroughly mashed overripe bananas.

Directions: Mix bananas with oil/sugar. Oil one standard or two small loaf pans, (or six mini-loafs). Stir dry ingredients into wet ingredients; stir until all is moist. Immediately put the batter in the pans and bake at 350 degrees for 40 minutes to an hour depending on loaf size.

Cool on rack. Serve with fresh banana slices, a dollop of almond or soy yogurt, or even coconut whipped cream. Yum!

*Ener-G Egg Replacer works well in most recipes. It can be purchased at natural foods stores or via the Ener-G website.

REFERENCES

1. Kristeller, J. and Wolever, R. 2013. "Sheets V. Mindfulness-Based Eating Awareness Training (MB-EAT) for Binge Eating: A Randomized Clinical Trial." *Mindfulness.* DOI 10.1007/s12671-012-0179-1.
2. Schmidt, L. 2014. "Sustainable Living and Conscious Eating." In *Beyond Stress: Strategies for Blissful Living,* ed. Napoli, M. Dubuque, IA: Kendall Hunt.
3. Graham, D. J., and Laska, M. N. 2012. "Nutrition Label Use Partially Mediates the Relationship Between Attitude Toward Healthy Eating and Overall Dietary Quality Among College Students." *Journal of the Academy of Nutrition and Dietetics* 112 (3), pp. 414–418.
4. Epel, E. S., Tomiyama, A. J., and Dallman, M. F. 2012. "Stress and Reward Neural Networks, Eating, and Obesity." In *Food and Addiction: A Comprehensive Handbook.* New York, NY: Oxford University Press(Laraia).
5. Schlosser, E. 2001. *Fast Food Nation: The Dark Side of the All-American Meal.* Boston: Houghton Mifflin.
6. Bowman, S. A., Gortmaker, S. L., Ebbeling, C. B., Pereira, M. A., and Ludwig, D. S. 2004. "Effects of Fast-Food Consumption on Energy Intake and Diet Quality Among Children in a National Household Survey." *Pediatrics* 113 (1), pp. 112–118.
7. Kong, A., Beresford, A. A., Alfano, C., Foster-Schubert, K., Neuhouser, M. L., Johnson, D., Duggan, C., Wang, C., and Xiao, L. J. "Self-Monitoring and Eating-Related Behaviors Are Associated with 12-Month Weight Loss in Postmenopausal Overweight-to-Obese Women." *Journal of the Academy of Nutrition and Dietetics* 112, pp. 1428–1435.
8. National Institutes of Health. "Sweet Stuff: How Sugar and Sweeteners Affect Your Health." [April 4, 2015]. Available from: http://newsinhealth.nih.gov/issue/oct2014/feature1.
9. US Department of Agriculture. "Empty Calories." *Myplate.gov.* [April 4, 2015]. Available from: http://www.choosemyplate.gov/weight-management-calories/calories/empty-calories.html.
10. "The Mindful Nutritionist." YouTube. [April 4, 2015]. Available from: https://www.youtube.com/channel/UCDrgYs4qKVNMSadsxLlbCbg.
11. Nordlee, J. A., Taylor, S. L., Townsend, J. A. et al. 1996. "Identification of a Brazil-nut Allergen in Transgenic Soybeans." *New England Journal of Medicine* 334 (11), pp. 688–692.
12. American Academy of Environmental Medicine. 2009. "Genetically Modified Foods." [April 4, 2015]. Available from: http://www.aaemonline.org/gmopost.html.
13. http://www.ncbi.nlm.nih.gov/pmc/articles/PMC3662288/pdf/permj17_2p0061.pdf.
14. US Department of Health. 2015. "Dietary Guidelines for Americans".[April 4, 2015]. Available from: http://www.health.gov/dietaryguidelines/2015.asp#qanda.
15. Pollan, M. 2006. *The Omivore's Dilemma.* New York, NY: Penguin Books.
16. Chah, A. 2002. *Food for the Heart: Collected Teachings of Ajahn Chah.* Boston: Wisdom. p. 236.
17. Bays, J. 2009. *Mindful Eating: A Guide to Rediscovering a Healthy and Joyful Relationship with Food.* Boston: Shambala Press.

MINDFUL EATING REFLECTION JOURNAL

1. Acknowledge
Describe your experience; what did you choose to eat?

2. Intentional Attention

Describe what you noticed during your mindful eating practice.

BREATH:	
BODY:	
EMOTIONS:	
THOUGHTS:	
SENSES:	

3. Accept Without Judgment
Describe judgment; acceptance

4. Choose Your Experience
Intention/willingness; new perspective

5. Mindful Meditation/Mindful Eating Experience (Mindful Practice)
What did you notice about your meditation experience this week?

MINDFUL EATING WEEKLY QUIZ

This is a brief snapshot of your mindful eating skills. It is to help you to identify which skills you may want to change or enhance. Circle the best answer. Don't forget to notice what you already do well. After you complete this quiz, write down a mindful eating goal for the week.

Take this quiz each week of the course.

1. I tend to stop eating when I am full				
⬅️➡️				
All of the time	Most of the time	Occasionally	Sometimes	Almost Never
2. I eat when I am hungry rather than when I feel emotional				
All of the time	Most of the time	Occasionally	Sometimes	Almost Never
3. I try not to "pick" at food				
All of the time	Most of the time	Occasionally	Sometimes	Almost Never
4. I taste each bite before reaching for the next				
All of the time	Most of the time	Occasionally	Sometimes	Almost Never
5. When I eat, I think about how nourishing the food is for my body				
All of the time	Most of the time	Occasionally	Sometimes	Almost Never
6. I am nonjudgmental of myself, my body and when I accidentally overeat				
All of the time	Most of the time	Occasionally	Sometimes	Almost Never
7. I don't multitask while I eat. When I eat, I just eat and focus on the food in front of me				
All of the time	Most of the time	Occasionally	Sometimes	Almost Never
8. I don't have to eat everything on my plate, I can leave what I don't want				
All of the time	Most of the time	Occasionally	Sometimes	Almost Never
9. I tend to eat slowly, chewing each bite				
All of the time	Most of the time	Occasionally	Sometimes	Almost Never
10. I recognize when I slip into mindless eating (zoned out, popping food into my mouth)				
All of the time	Most of the time	Occasionally	Sometimes	Almost Never
List your Mindful Eating Goals: (ex: learn to be more present when I eat, slow down, stop when I'm full)				